Your First Ye

Guidelines for Success

Fifth Edition

Richard D. Kellough

Professor Emeritus
California State University, Sacramento

Boston, Massachusetts
Columbus, Ohio

10 9 8 7 6 5 4
ISBN-13: 978-0-13-714943-8
ISBN-10: 0-13-714943-3

CONTENTS[+],[*]

[+]See page viii for an alternate order of contents for use in a preservice instructional methods course
[*]New to this edition

NOTE: Every effort has been made to provide accurate and current Internet addresses in this book. During 2006, the author personally visited each Internet site recommended. However, the Internet and information posted on it are constantly changing, so it is inevitable that some addresses in this book will change.

ALTERNATE ORDER OF CONTENTS

Recommended for Use in a Preservice Instructional Methods Course

TEACHER PREP

MERRILL
PRENTICE HALL

Teacher Preparation Classroom

Your Class. Their Careers. Our Future. Will your students be prepared?

We invite you to explore our new, innovative and engaging website and all that it has to offer you, your course, and tomorrow's educators! Preview this site today at **www.prenhall.com/teacherprep/demo**. Just click on "go" on the login page to begin your exploration.

Organized around the major courses pre-service teachers take, the Teacher Preparation site provides media, student/teacher artifacts, strategies, research articles, and other resources to equip your students with the quality tools needed to excel in their courses and prepare them for their first classroom.

This ultimate on-line education resource will provide you and your students access to:

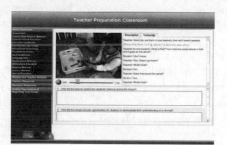

Online Video Library More than 250 video clips—each tied to a course topic and framed by learning goals and Praxis-type questions—capture real teachers and students working in real classrooms.

Student and Teacher Artifacts More than 200 student and teacher classroom artifacts—each tied to a course topic and framed by learning goals and application questions—provide a wealth of materials and experiences to help make your students ovserve children's developmental learning.

Lesson Plan Builder Offers step-by-step guidelines and lesson plan examples to support students as they learn to build high quality lesson plans.

Research Articles Over 500 articles from ASCD's renowned journal, *Educational Leadership*. The site also includes *Research Navigator*, a searchable database of additional educational journals.

Teaching Strategies Over 500 research supported instructional strategies appropriate for a wide range of grade levels and content areas.

Licensure and Career Tools Resources devoted to helping your students pass their licensure exam, learn standards, law, and public policies, plan a teaching portfolio, and survive their first year of teaching.

How to ORDER *Teacher Prep* for you and your students:
For students to receive a *Teacher Prep* Access Code with this text, the instructor **must** provide a special value pack ISBN number on their textbook order form. To receive this special ISBN, please email: **Merrill.marketing@pearsoned.com** and provide the following information:
- Name and Affiliation
- Author/Title/Edition of Merrill text

Upon ordering *Teacher Prep* for their students, instructors will be given a lifetime *Teacher Prep* Access Code.

PROLOGUE

I know of no profession potentially any more intrinsically rewarding than that of teaching. However, for a public school classroom teacher, the first year of teaching or the beginning year at a new school can be an extremely difficult and intimidating experience.

Many schools provide new teachers with a planned program of new-teacher induction and mentoring. If your school does not provide a program, then you will need to assert yourself and build a network of supporters. For a teacher without support, the first year can be overwhelming. Coupled with low starting pay, large class sizes, and mounting financial crises, it is little wonder that so many teachers become disenchanted with the profession and exit it within a few years.

By providing practical guidelines for topics that concern most beginning teachers, this little book provides a bit of a haven of help to prevent your becoming too frustrated and discouraged. It is my hope that it will aid in making your first year of teaching one that is intrinsically rewarding for you and emotionally and academically successful for you and your students.

You are beginning a career during which you will be in a perpetual mode of reflection and learning. Be kind to yourself; do not expect immediate mastery. Nobody truly knowledgeable about it ever said that good teaching was easy. Becoming a good teacher takes time, commitment, concentrated effort, and just plain hard work. The task of becoming a truly competent classroom teacher is a continuous challenge and never boring.

Perhaps the most important guideline of all is to value yourself and what you are doing. The first year of teaching is full of highs and lows, with few days in-between or neutral. There are days when you realize teaching is wonderful, and there are days where you are stressed to the max. Let yourself know when you're doing a good job, and when you are feeling low, remember that things can always improve. And never forget that even on your worst days you still are some student's best hope.

Although guidelines presented in this book are mostly grade-level and subject matter neutral, depending on your own particular teaching situation, you will personally find some to be more relevant than are others. Teaching is as much an art as it is a science; this book is not a magic bag of recipes that will work for every teacher in every situation. As general guidelines for success during your first year of teaching, it does represent the best from recent research and from current practice. If you find that your interest is piqued by a particular guideline, you may learn more about that topic by referring to additional resources such as those listed beginning on page 95.

ACCOMMODATING STUDENT DIFFERENCES: RECOGNIZING AND WORKING WITH SPECIFIC LEARNERS

You are probably quite aware that the variety of individual differences among students in your classroom requires that you use teaching strategies that to some degree or another accommodate those differences. To do that well, you should be able to answer yes to each of the four questions found in Figure 1.

Figure 1: Questions for teacher reflection about planning and accommodating for student differences

---

- Do I establish a classroom climate in which *all* students feel welcome, that they can learn, and that I support them in doing so?
- Do I use techniques that emphasize cooperative and social-interactive learning?
- Do I build on students' individual experiences, conceptions, learning styles, learning capacities, and learning modalities?
- Do I use techniques that have proven successful for students of specific differences?

The importance of building your skills in each of the four areas or categories represented by those questions is likely now quite apparent to you, and is a process that began, or should have, during your teacher training and will continue throughout your professional career. Specific guidelines that follow will serve as helpful reminders. If you are still unclear as to the meaning of any of the four questions, then you need to investigate the topic to a depth beyond that provided by this little book (for that in-depth assistance see the suggested readings at the end of this book).

Students with Special Needs

Students with special needs (referred to also as students with exceptionalities) include those with disabling conditions or impairments in any one or more of the following categories: mental retardation, hearing, speech or language, visual, emotional, orthopedic, autism, traumatic brain injury, other health impairment, or specific learning disabilities. To receive special education services, a child must have a disability in one or more of the categories, and by reason thereof, the child needs special education and related services. In other words, not all children who have a disability need services available via special education. For example, a child with a hearing impairment would be entitled to special services when the impairment is so severe that the child cannot understand what is being said even when the child is equipped with a hearing aid.

Although the guidelines represented by the paragraphs that follow are important for teaching all students, they are especially important for working with special needs students.

- Adapting and modifying materials and procedures to the special needs of each student. For example, a student who has extreme difficulty sitting still for more than a few minutes will need planned changes in learning activities. When establishing student seating arrangements in the classroom, give preference to students according to their special needs. Try to incorporate into lessons activities that engage all learning modalities—visual, auditory, tactile, and kinesthetic. Be flexible in your classroom procedures. For example, allow the use of recorders for note taking and test taking when students have trouble with the written language.

- Exercising your withitness, monitoring students for signs of restlessness, frustration, anxiety, and off-task behaviors. Be ready to reassign individual learners to different activities as the situation warrants.

- Familiarizing yourself with exactly what the special needs of each learner are. Privately ask the special needs student whether there is anything he or she would like for you to know and that you specifically can do to facilitate his or her learning.

- Having all students maintain assignments for the week or some other period of time in an assignment book or in a folder kept in their notebooks. Post assignments in a special place in the classroom (and perhaps on the school's web site) and frequently remind students of assignments and deadlines.

- Maintaining consistency in your expectations and in your responses. Special needs learners, particularly, can become frustrated when they do not understand a teacher's expectations and when they cannot depend on a teacher's reactions.

- Planning interesting activities to bridge learning, activities that help students connect what is being learned with their real world experiences.

- Providing for and teaching toward student success. Offer students activities and experiences that ensure each student's success and mastery at some level. Use of student portfolios can give evidence of progress and help in building student confidence and self-esteem.

- Providing help in the organization of students' learning. For example, give instruction in the organization of notes and notebooks. Have a three-hole punch available in the classroom so students can place their papers into their notebooks immediately, thus avoiding disorganization and the loss of papers. During class presentations, use an overhead projector with transparencies; students who need more time can then copy material from the transparencies. Ask students to read their notes aloud to each other in small groups, thereby aiding their recall and understanding, and encouraging them to take notes for meaning rather than for rote learning. Encourage and provide for peer support, peer tutoring or coaching, and cross-age teaching. Ensure the special needs learner is included in all class activities to the fullest extent possible.

- Providing high structure and clear expectations by defining the learning objectives in behavioral terms. Teach students the correct procedures for everything. Break complex learning into simpler components, moving from the most concrete to the abstract, rather than the other way around. Check frequently for student understanding of instructions and procedures, and for comprehension of content.

Use computers and other self-correcting materials for drill and practice and for provision of immediate, constructive, and private feedback to the student.

- Providing scaffolded instruction, that is, give each student as much guided or coached practice as time allows. Provide time in class for students to work on assignments and projects. During this time, you can monitor the work of each student while looking for misconceptions, thus ensuring students get started on the right track.

Students of Diversity and Differences

You must quickly determine the language and ethnic groups represented by the students in your classroom. A major problem for recent newcomers, as well as some ethnic groups, is learning a second (or third or fourth) language. While in many schools it is not uncommon for more than half the students to come from homes where the spoken language is not English, standard English is a necessity in most communities of this country if a person is to become vocationally successful and enjoy a full life. Learning to communicate reasonably well in English can take an immigrant child at least a year and probably longer, and from three to seven years to catch up academically in English. By default, then, an increasing percentage of public school teachers in the United States are teachers of English language learning (ELL). Helpful to the success of teaching students who are ELLs are the demonstration of respect for students' cultural backgrounds, long-term teacher–student cohorts (such as those in looping), and the use of active and cooperative learning.

There are numerous programs specially designed for English language learners. Most use the acronym LEP (limited English proficiency) with five number levels, from LEP 1 which designates non-English-speaking (although the student may understand single sentences and speak simple words or phrases in English) to LEP 5, sometimes designated FEP (fluent English proficiency), for the student who is fully fluent in English, although the student's overall academic achievement may still be less than desired because of language or cultural differences.

Some schools use a "pullout" approach, where a portion of the student's school time is spent in special bilingual classes and the rest of the time the student is placed in regular classrooms. In some schools, LEP students are placed in academic classrooms that use a simplified or "sheltered" English approach. For schools that participate in NCLB legislation (they accept federal funding), ELLs as a subgroup must meet Adequate Yearly Progress (AYP) targets for reading and mathematics proficiency and they must meet Annual Measurable Achievement Objectives (AMAOs) for English language proficiency.

Regardless of the program and its source of funding, specific techniques recommended for teaching ELL students include (Fitzgerald & Graves, 2005; Meyer, 2000; Miller & Endo, 2004; Walling, 1993):

- Assisting the child in learning how to deal with the anxiety caused by "language shock," that is, from not knowing or understanding well the language of the child's new country.

3

- Allowing more time for learning activities than one normally would.
- Allowing time for translation by a classroom aide or by a classmate and allowing time for dialogue to clarify meaning, encouraging the students to transfer into English what they already know in their native language.
- Avoiding jargon or idioms that might be misunderstood.
- Building upon what the students already have experienced and know.
- Dividing complex or extended language discourse into smaller, more manageable units.
- Encouraging student writing, such as by using student journals or by using blogs (see the Teaching in Practice scenario on page 57).
- Giving directions in a variety of ways.
- Giving special attention to keywords that convey meaning and writing them on the board.
- Helping students learn the vocabulary. Assist the ELL students in learning two vocabulary sets: the regular English vocabulary needed for learning and the new vocabulary introduced by the subject content. For example, while learning science a student is dealing with both the regular English language vocabulary and the special vocabulary of science.
- Involving parents or guardians or siblings. Students whose primary language is not English may have other differences about which you will also need to become knowledgeable. These differences are related to culture, customs, family life, and expectations. To be most successful in working with language-minority students, you should learn as much as possible about each student. Parents (or guardians) of new immigrant children are usually truly concerned about the education of their children and may be very interested in cooperating with you in any way possible.
- Planning for and using all learning modalities by using auditory, visual, tactile, and kinesthetic learning activities.
- Presenting instruction that is concrete (least abstract) and that includes the most direct learning experiences possible.
- Providing scaffolded reading experiences, that is a framework of activities for use in prereading (such as preteaching vocabulary and predicting outcomes), during-reading (such as guided reading and silent reading activities), and postreading (such as playacting and writing), of any genre of text.
- Reading written directions aloud, and then writing the directions on the board.
- Reducing the cognitive load while still maintaining high expectations for the learning of each learner.
- Speaking clearly and naturally but at a slower than normal pace.
- Treating the ELLs, their homes and communities, and their primary languages and cultures with respect, and not with negative judgments.
- Using a variety of examples and observable models.
- Using simplified vocabulary without talking down to students

- Using small-group cooperative learning. Cooperative learning strategies are particularly effective with language-minority students because they provide opportunities for students to produce language in a setting less threatening than is speaking before the entire class.
- Using the benefits afforded by modern technology. For example, computer networking allows students to write and communicate with peers from around the world as well as participate in "publishing" their classroom work.

ENGAGING A NEW GENERATION OF CITIZENS

Immigrant students might find the U.S. concept of democracy difficult to grasp. How can a school make students with different languages, ethnicities, races, and complex personal histories understand the importance of the democratic tradition even as they pursue individual dreams of achievement?

The answer: Make learning student-centered and activity- and project-based. Allow immigrant students to communicate in both English and native languages and work in small groups to create a play, collaborate on a work of art, or hash out a mathematical concept.

Rick Allen (2003)

ADDITIONAL GUIDELINES FOR WORKING WITH STUDENTS OF DIVERSE BACKGROUNDS

To be compatible with, and be able to teach, students who come from backgrounds different from yours, you need to believe that, given adequate support, all students *can* learn—regardless of gender, social class, physical characteristics, language, religion, and ethnic or cultural backgrounds. You also need to develop special skills that include those in the following guidelines.

- Building the learning around students' individual learning styles. To the extent possible, personalize learning for each student, much like what is done by using the Individualized Education Plan (IEP) with special needs learners.
- Establishing and maintain high expectations, although not necessarily the same expectations, for each student. Both you and your students must understand intelligence is not a fixed entity, but a set of characteristics that—through a feeling of "I can" and with proper coaching—can be developed.
- Teaching individuals by using a variety of strategies to achieve an objective or by using a number of different objectives at the same time (multilevel teaching).
- Using techniques that emphasize collaborative and cooperative learning—that deemphasize competitive learning.

Students Who Take More Time but Are Willing to Try

Students who are slower to learn typically fall into one of two categories: (1) those who try to learn but simply need more time to do it, and (2) those who do not try, referred to variously as underachievers or recalcitrant or reluctant learners. Practices that work well with students of one category are often not those that work well with those of the second—making life difficult for a teacher of 28 students, half who try and half who don't (Kellough, 1970). It is worse still for a teacher of a group of 25 or so students, some who try but need time, one or two who learn regardless, 2 or 3 who have special needs but not the same special needs, a few LEP students, and several who not only seem unwilling to try but who are also disruptive in the classroom. And, by the way, this last example is probably closer to reality for the vast majority of teachers of today's public schools.

> Just because a student is slow to learn doesn't mean the student is less intelligent; some students just plain take longer, for any number of reasons.

The following guidelines may be helpful when working with a student who is slow but willing to try:

- Adjusting the instruction to the student's preferred learning style, which may be different from yours and from other students in the group.
- Being less concerned with the amount of content coverage than with the student's successful understanding of content that is covered. Teach toward mastery (although this may be antagonistic to modern emphasis on improved student scores on high-stakes assessment tests).
- Discovering something the student does exceptionally well, or a special interest, and try and connect the student's learning with that.
- Emphasizing basic communication skills, such as speaking, listening, reading, and writing, to ensure the student's skills in these areas are sufficient for learning the intended content.
- Getting to know each student, at least well enough that you have empathy for where the person is coming from. For example, many adolescents from high-poverty inner-city neighborhoods feel hopeless that they will be able to improve their lives (Bolland, 2003). Commit yourself to helping them understand the power of education in finding their way out of such feelings of hopelessness.
- Helping the student learn content in small sequential steps with frequent checks for comprehension. Use instructional scaffolding.
- If necessary, helping the student to improve his or her reading skills, such as pronunciation and word meanings.
- If you are using a single textbook, being certain the reading level is adequate for the student; if it is not, then for that student use other more appropriate reading materials. Many teachers maintain a variety of optional texts in their classroom just for this purpose.

- Maximizing the use of in-class, on-task work and cooperative learning, with close monitoring of the student's progress. Avoid relying much on successful completion of traditional out-of-class assignments unless you can supply coaching to the student in the classroom.
- Varying the instructional strategies, using a variety of activities to engage the visual, verbal, tactile, and kinesthetic modalities.
- When appropriate, using frequent positive reinforcement, with the intention of building the student's confidence and self-esteem.

Recalcitrant Learners

For working with recalcitrant learners, you can use many of the same guidelines from the preceding list, except you should understand that the reasons for these students' behaviors may be quite different from those for the other category of slow learners. Slower-learning students who are willing to try may be slow because of their learning style, because of genetic factors, or a combination of those and any number of other reasons. They are simply slower at learning. But they can and will learn. Recalcitrant learners, on the other hand, may be generally quick and bright thinkers but reluctant even to try because of a history of failure, a history of boredom with school, low confidence level for academic work, a poor self-concept, severe personal problems that distract from school, or any variety and combination of reasons, many of which are emotional/psychological in nature.

Whatever the case, a student identified as being a slow or recalcitrant learner might, in fact, be quite gifted or talented in some way, but because of personal problems, have a history of increasingly poor school attendance, poor attention to schoolwork, poor self-confidence, and an attitude problem. With those factors in mind, consider the following guidelines when working with recalcitrant learners:

- As the school year begins, learning as much about each student as you can. Be cautious in how you do it, though, because many of these students will be suspicious of any interest you show in them. Be businesslike, trusting, genuinely interested, and patient. A second caution: although you learn as much as possible about each student, what has happened in the past is history. Use the information not as ammunition, something to be held against the student, but as insight to help you work more productively with the student.
- Avoiding lecturing to these students; it won't work, at least not for a while.
- Early in the school term, preferably with the help of adult volunteers (e.g., using professional community members as mentors has worked well at helping change the student's attitude from rebellion to one of hope, challenge, and success), work out a personalized education program with each student.
- Engaging the students in learning by using interactive media, such as the Internet.
- Engaging the students in active learning with real-world problem solving and perhaps community service projects (see the many examples later in this book in the list of motivational strategies).

- Forget about trying to "cover the subject matter," concentrating instead on student learning of some things well. Practice mastery (although this may go against the grain of modern emphasis on improved student scores on high-stakes achievement tests). A good procedure is to use thematic teaching and divide the theme into short segments. Because school attendance for these students is sometimes sporadic, try personalizing their assignments so they can pick up where they left off and move through the course in an orderly fashion even when they have been absent excessively. Try assuring some degree of success for each student.

- Helping students develop their studying and learning skills, such as concentrating, remembering, and comprehension. Mnemonics, for example, is a device these students respond to positively; they are often quick and creative in inventing their own.

- If you are using a single textbook, see if the reading level is appropriate; if it is not, then for that student discard the book and select other more appropriate reading materials.

- Making sure your classroom procedures and rules are understood at the beginning of the school term and being consistent about following them.

- Maximizing the use of in-class, on-task work and cooperative learning, with close monitoring of the student's progress. Do not rely on successful completion of traditional out-of-class assignments unless the student receives coached guidance from you before leaving your classroom.

- Using simple language in the classroom. Be concerned less about the words the students use and the way they use them and more about the ideas they are expressing. Let the students use their own idioms without carping too much on grammar and syntax. Always take care, though, to model proper and professional English yourself.

- When appropriate, using frequent positive reinforcement, with the intention of increasing the student's sense of personal worth. When using praise for reinforcement, however, try to direct your praise to the deed rather than the student.

ATTAINING CREDIBILITY WITH STUDENTS: TEACHER ATTITUDE AND MODELING BEHAVIORS

You probably don't need to be told that students enjoy and learn better from a teacher who is positive and optimistic, encouraging, nurturing, and happy rather than from a teacher who is negative and pessimistic, discouraging, uninterested, and grumpy.

Additionally, to build and maintain credibility with students your behaviors should model the very behaviors expected of the students. For example,

- If you expect students to demonstrate regular and punctual attendance, then you should be punctual and regular

- If you expect students to have their work done on time, then you should do likewise, returning their work promptly after reading, assessing, and recording it

- If you expect students to have their materials each day for learning, then you, too, must be prepared each day
- If you expect students to demonstrate cooperative behavior and respect for others, then you must do likewise
- If you expect students to maintain an open and inquisitive mind, to demonstrate critical thinking, and to use proper communication skills, then you will do likewise

BEYOND TEACHING: A TEACHER IS INTERESTING BECAUSE THE TEACHER HAS A LIFE OUTSIDE SCHOOL

You should clearly demonstrate an interest in the activities of the students and the many aspects of the school and its surrounding community. In addition, a wide range of interests outside school will help you sustain your good health, energy, and enthusiasm for teaching. A teacher is interesting because of his or her interests; a teacher with varied interests more often motivates and captures the attention of more students. A teacher with no interests outside his or her subject and the classroom is likely a dull or soon-to-be burned out teacher.

First Year of Teaching: Not the Best Time to Assume New Personal and Social Commitments and Responsibilities

On the other hand, because you will be so busy, your first teaching year may not be the best time to initiate graduate study or to assume major new social obligations and responsibilities. For example, you may want to think twice before planning a wedding or starting a family during your first year of teaching.

COLLEAGUES, ADMINISTRATORS, AND SUPPORT STAFF: YOUR PROFESSIONAL NETWORK

It is advisable to establish from the faculty at least one good friend. If you are a member of a teaching team, then at least one member of your team should be a friend with whom you can talk openly.

In many school districts, new teachers are automatically assigned to mentor teachers for their first, and sometimes second, year, as a program of induction. The mentor might or might not be a teacher from your school. The mentor's responsibility is to periodically observe, coach, and provide support to the beginning teacher.

Mentor: Sometimes It's Good to Have More Than One

It frequently is beneficial to have several mentors, one who is your official mentor, and then others who are unofficial and perhaps even only occasional mentors. For example, I think it is a good idea to establish a collegial friendship with another first-year teacher, and it doesn't necessarily need to be someone who is at your school, but merely someone with whom you can talk freely and who is likely to be sharing similar experiences and feelings. A school administrator can be helpful toward guiding your understandings of school policies and how to best prepare for special events and end-of-term requirements. A teacher who is teaching the same subject or grade level or a similar group of students as you can be a valuable resource for specific matters of curriculum and instruction. Maintain a small notebook of specific questions you want to ask the various members of your professional network, and then don't hesitate to ask them.

An Expert Among Professionals

Because of some special skill or knowledge, beginning teachers sometimes feel pressured to help veteran teachers learn new skills or strategies. The request for help is made with the best of intention; it's just that veterans often have forgotten what the time demands on a beginning teacher can be like. For a new teacher who wants to feel accepted, it is sometimes difficult to say no to such requests. My advice: Be prepared for such requests and try to make time to help; just be careful to not overtax yourself. On the other hand, don't be afraid to say no; professionals will understand.

Envious Colleagues

Envious colleagues sometimes ostracize teachers who—because of their enthusiasm, creativity, positivism, and fresh ideas—try to accomplish great things with their students. (See the article by J.M. Wood [2000] in the suggested readings in the back of this book.) Unfortunately, in too many instances, after a few years, these creative teachers leave their respective schools and even the profession. Be prepared; if you are creative and enthusiastic about your teaching, there may be jealousy displayed by colleagues who are less enthusiastic, less successful, or burned out. My advice: Try to ignore them and focus on your students and your work. To the extent possible, surround yourself with the most positive and supportive people.

Staff Should Be Valuable Members of Your Support Network

Two important persons at the school are the head custodian and the principal's secretary. If possible, include those persons in your network of professional friends. You will want to identify and include others at your school, such as members of the cafeteria staff and security personnel.

Sharing a Common Purpose

The best schools and the best teachers provide a constructive and positive environment for learning, demonstrating optimism for the learning of each and every student.

For a student, nothing at school is more satisfying than having a teacher who demonstrates confidence in that student's abilities. Unfortunately, for some students, a teacher's show of confidence may be the only positive indicator that student ever receives. Each of us can recall with admiration a teacher (or other significant person) who demonstrated confidence in our ability to accomplish seemingly formidable tasks. A competent teacher demonstrates this confidence with each student. Although this doesn't mean that you must personally like every student with whom you will ever come into contact, it does mean that you accept each as a person of dignity and who is worthy of receiving your respect, your professional skills, and your best effort.

Seek Help Whenever You Feel a Perceived Need—Don't Wait Too Long

Sometimes beginning teachers ask themselves just when they should ask for help, or how should they ask, or who. My answer to the first part is to ask exactly when you feel a need for help—don't wait. To the second part, ask straightforward questions. And to the final part, don't necessarily keep seeking help from the same person but rather from the right person for the specific question, the very reason you need a network of professional friends rather than one person.

CURRICULUM MATTERS AND CONCERNS

The accumulation of bits and pieces of information is at the lowest end of a spectrum of types of learning. For higher levels of thinking and doing, for learning that is most meaningful and longest lasting, the results of research support using (a) a curriculum where subjects are integrated and (b) instructional techniques that involve the learners in social interactive (student-centered) learning, such as cooperative group learning, inquiry, project-based learning, peer tutoring, and cross-age teaching.

Teaching Both Children and the Content Standards: An Oxymoron?

A concern of many beginning teachers (and veterans, too) is that of discovering how to use more student-centered instruction as opposed to teacher-centered instruction (e.g., lecture and recitation) and still effectively teach the mandated or expected curriculum so that student achievement matches the expected outcome standards of the various content areas. Elementary teachers in particular grapple for answers to the question of how to find the time to teach all the required content areas of the curriculum. At all levels—elementary, middle, and high school—teachers struggle with how to use more *hands-on* (i.e., doing it) and *minds-on* (i.e., thinking about what one is doing) learning (which takes more time and materials) and still cover the expected and even mandated curriculum. (By the way, doing it without thinking about it is *not* learning.) One key to success in accomplishing this is via the use of some level of curriculum integration.

Integrating the Subjects: More Like Real Life

When speaking of curriculum integration, it is easy to be confused by the plethora of terms that are used, such as *integrated studies, thematic instruction, multidisciplinary teaching, interdisciplinary curriculum,* and *interdisciplinary thematic instruction.* In essence, regardless of which term is used, the reference is to the same thing and that is to curriculum that is integrated. An integrated curriculum approach may not necessarily be the best approach for every school or the best for all learning for every student, nor is it necessarily the manner by which every teacher should or must always plan and teach. As evidenced by practice, the truth of this statement becomes obvious.

In attempts to help students connect their learning with their life experiences, efforts fall at various places on a continuum of sophistication and complexity, from the least integrated instruction (level 1) to the most integrated (level 5) (Kellough et al., 1996). What follows is presented to assist your understanding only; it is not my intention to imply that for every teacher or every program or school, one level is any more appropriate or effective than another. The fact is that there are various interpretations and/or modifications to curriculum integration, and each teacher must make his or her own decisions about the use.

Level 1 Curriculum Integration. Level 1 curriculum integration is the traditional organization of curriculum and classroom instruction, in which teachers plan and arrange the subject-specific scope and sequence in the format of topic outlines. If there is an attempt to help students connect their learning and their experiences, then it is up to individual classroom teachers to do it. An elementary or middle school student in a school and classroom that has subject-specific instruction at varying times of the day (e.g., reading and language arts at 8:00, mathematics at 9:00, social studies at 10:30, and so on) from one or more teachers is likely learning at a level 1 instructional environment, especially when what is being learned in one subject has little or no connection with content being learned in another. The same applies to a high school student who moves during the school day from classroom to classroom, teacher to teacher, subject to subject, one topic to another; he or she is likely learning at a level 1 instructional environment. A topic in science, for example, might be "earthquakes." A related topic in social studies might be "the social consequences of natural disasters." These two topics may or may not be studied by a student at the same time.

Level 2 Curriculum Integration. If the same students are learning English/language arts, or social studies/history, or mathematics, or science using a thematic approach rather than a topic outline, then they are learning at level 2. At this level, themes for one discipline are not necessarily planned and coordinated to correspond or integrate with themes of another or to be taught simultaneously. At level 2, the students may have some input into the decision-making involved in planning themes and content from various disciplines. Before going further in this discussion of the levels of curriculum integration, let's stop and consider what is a topic and what is a theme.

Topic versus theme. The difference between a topic and what is a theme is not always clear. For example, whereas "earthquakes" and "social consequences of natural disasters" are topics, "natural disasters" could be the theme or umbrella under which these two topics could fall. In addition, themes are likely to be problem-based

12

statements or questions; they often result in a product and are longer in duration than are topics. A theme is the point, the message, or the idea that underlies a study. When compared to a topic, a theme is more dynamic; the theme explains the significance of the study. It communicates to the student what the experience means. Although organized around one theme, many topics make up an ITU (interdisciplinary thematic unit). Often the theme of a study becomes clearer to students when an overall guiding question is presented and discussed, such as "What happens in and to our community after a natural disaster?"

Level 3 Curriculum Integration. When the same students are learning two or more of their core subjects (English/language arts, social studies/history, mathematics, and science) around a common theme, such as the theme "natural disasters," from one or more teachers, they are then learning at level 3 curriculum integration. At this level, teachers agree on a common theme, and then they *separately* deal with that theme in their individual disciplines, usually at the same time during the school year. So what the student is learning from a teacher in one class is related to and coordinated with what the student is concurrently learning from another or several others. At level 3, students may have some input into the decision making involved in selecting and planning themes and content. Some writers may refer to levels 2 or 3 as *coordinated or parallel curriculum.*

Level 4 Curriculum Integration. When teachers and students collaborate on a common theme and its content and when discipline boundaries begin to disappear as teachers teach about this common theme, either solo or as an interdisciplinary teaching team, level 4 integration is achieved.

Level 5 Curriculum Integration. When teachers and their students have collaborated on a common theme and its content, and discipline boundaries are truly indistinct during instruction, and teachers of several grade levels and of various subjects teach toward student understanding of aspects of the common theme, then this is level 5, an *integrated thematic approach.*

Detailed guidelines for integrating topics and for planning and developing an ITU are available in Roberts and Kellough, *A Guide to Developing an Interdisciplinary Thematic Unit* (2008), and in several other sources found in the suggested readings at the end of this book.

Cooperative Learning: Don't Give Up Before Experiencing Its Benefits

Sometimes, when they think they are using cooperative learning groups (CLGs), teachers have difficulty and either give up trying to use the strategy or simply tell students to divide into groups for an activity and call it cooperative learning. For the strategy to work, each student must be given training in and have acquired basic skills in interaction and group processing. Students must realize that progress in individual achievement rests with that of their group.

The cooperative learning group is a heterogeneous group (i.e., mixed according to one or more criteria, such as ability or skill level, ethnicity, learning style, learning capacity, gender, and language proficiency) of three to six students who work together in a teacher- or student-directed setting, emphasizing support for one another. Often, a CLG consists of four students of mixed ability, learning styles, gender, and ethnicity, with each member of the group assuming a particular role. Teachers usually change the membership of each group several to many times during the year. The theory of cooperative learning is that when small groups of students of mixed backgrounds, learning styles, and capabilities work together toward a common goal, members of the group increase their friendship and respect for one another. As a consequence, each individual's self-esteem is enhanced, students are more motivated to participate in higher order thinking, and academic achievement is accomplished.

When the process of using CLGs is well planned and managed, the outcomes of cooperative learning include improved communication and relationships of acceptance among students of differences, quality learning with fewer off-task behaviors, and increased academic achievement.

For CLGs to work well, advanced planning and effective management are critically important. Students must be instructed in the necessary skills for group learning. Each student must be assigned a responsible role (specific function) within the group and be held accountable for fulfilling that responsibility. When a CLG activity is in process, groups must be continually monitored by the teacher for possible breakdown of this process within a group. When a potential breakdown is noticed, the teacher intervenes to help the group get back on track.

The roles should be rotated, either during the activity or from one time to the next. Although titles may vary, five typical roles are:

- *Group facilitator*—function is to keep the group on task
- *Materials manage*—function is to obtain, maintain, and return materials needed for the group to function
- *Recorder*—function is to record all group activities and processes and perhaps to periodically analyze how the group is doing
- *Reporter*—function is to report group processes and accomplishments to the teacher and/or to the entire class. When using groups of four members, the roles of recorder and reporter can easily be combined
- *Thinking monitor*—function is to identify and record the sequence and processes of the group's thinking.

It is important that students understand and perform their individual roles and that each member of the CLG performs her or his function as expected. No student should be allowed to ride on the coattails of the group. To emphasize significance and to reinforce the importance of each role, and to be able to recognize readily the role any student is assuming during CLG activity, one teacher made a trip to an office supplier and had permanent badges made for the various CLG roles. During CLGs, then, each student attaches the appropriate badge to her or his clothing.

Actually, for learning by CLGs to work, each member of the CLG must understand and assume two roles or responsibilities: the role he or she is assigned as a member of the group, and that of seeing that all others in the group are performing their roles. Sometimes this requires interpersonal skills that students have yet to learn or to learn well. This is where you, the teacher, must assume some responsibility. Simply placing students into CLGs and expecting each member and each group to function and to learn the expected outcomes may not work. In other words, skills of cooperation must be taught, learned, and practiced. If all your students have not yet learned the skills of cooperation, then you will have to teach them. This doesn't mean that if a group is not functioning, you immediately dissolve the group and reassign its members to new groups. Part of group learning is learning the process of how to resolve conflict. A group may require your assistance to solve a conflict. With your guidance the group should be able to discover the problem that is causing the conflict, identify some options, and mediate at least a temporary solution. If a particular skill is needed, then with your guidance students identify and learn that skill.

CLGs can be used for problem solving, investigations, opinion surveys, experiments, review, project work, test making, or almost any other instructional purpose. Just as you would for small-group work in general, you can use CLGs for most any purpose at any time, but as with any other instructional strategy, it should not be overused.

Group Grading: Not Recommended

The purpose of a cooperative learning group is for the group to learn, which means that individuals within a group must learn. Group achievement in learning, then, depends on the learning of individuals within the group. Rather than competing for rewards for achievement, members of the group cooperate with each other by helping each other to learn so the group reward will be a good one.

When the achievement of a CLG is recognized, group achievement is rewarded along with individual achievement. Remembering that the emphasis must be on peer support rather than peer pressure, you are advised to *avoid ever giving group grades*. Some teachers give bonus points to all members of a group to add to their individual scores when everyone in the group has reached preset criteria. In establishing preset standards, the standards can be different for individuals within a group, depending on each member's ability and past performance. Some teachers also give subjective grades to individual students on their role performance within the group. For determination of students' report card grades, individual student achievement is measured later through individual results on tests and other sources of data. The final grade is based on those sources and on the student's performance in the group.

Controversial Content and Issues: Unavoidable

Controversial content and issues abound in certain disciplines, for example in English/language arts, regarding whole language/phonics and regarding certain books (see Figure 2); in social studies, regarding values and moral issues; in science, regarding the inclusion of the topics biological evolution and creationism. As a general rule, if you have concern that a particular topic or activity might create controversy, it probably will. During your teaching career, you undoubtedly will need to make decisions about how you will handle such matters. When selecting content that might be controversial, consider the following paragraphs as guidelines.

Figure 2: Ten most frequently challenged books in 2005

1. *It's Perfectly Normal* by Robie H. Harris
2. *Forever* by Judy Blume
3. *The Catcher in the Rye* by J. D. Salinger
4. *The Chocolate War* by Robert Cormier
5. *Whale Talk* by Chris Crutcher
6. *Detour for Emmy* by Marilyn Reynolds
7. *What My Mother Doesn't Know* by Sonya Sones
8. *Captain Underpants* series by Dav Pilkey
9. *Crazy Lady!* by Jane Leslie Conly
10. *It's So Amazing!* by Robie H. Harris

Source: American Library Association.

Maintain a perspective with respect to your own goal, which is at the moment to retain your job and obtain tenure. While student teaching, probationary teaching is not necessarily the best time to become involved in controversy. If you communicate closely with your mentor (if you have one), your department or grade-level chair, and perhaps your school principal, you should be able to anticipate and prevent major problems dealing with controversial issues.

Sometimes, during normal discussion in the classroom, a controversial topic will emerge spontaneously, catching the teacher off guard. If this happens, think before saying anything. You may wish to postpone further discussion until you have had a chance to confer with members of your teaching team or other colleagues. Controversial topics can seem to arise from nowhere for any teacher, and this is perfectly normal. Young people are in the process of developing their moral and value systems, and they need and want to know how adults feel about issues that are important to them, particularly those adults they hold in esteem—their teachers. Young adolescents and teens need to discuss issues that are important to society, and there is absolutely nothing wrong with dealing in the classroom with those issues as long as certain guidelines are followed.

First, students should learn about all sides of an issue. Controversial issues are open-ended and should be treated as such. They do not have "right" answers or "correct" solutions. If they did, there would be no controversy. (An "issue" differs from a "problem" in that a problem generally has a solution, whereas an issue has many opinions and several alternative solutions.) Therefore, the focus should be on both process and content. A major goal is to show students how to deal with controversy and to mediate wise decisions on the basis of carefully considered information. Another goal is to help students learn how to disagree without being disagreeable—how to resolve conflict. To that end students need to learn the difference between conflicts that are destructive and those that can be constructive, in other words, to see that conflict (disagreement) can be healthy, that it can have value.

A third goal, of course, is to help students learn about the content of an issue so, when necessary, they can make decisions based on knowledge, not on ignorance.

Second, as with all lesson plans, topics that could lead to controversy should be well thought out ahead of time. Problems for a teacher are most likely to occur when the plan has not been well conceived and designed.

Third, at some point all persons directly involved in an issue have a right to input: students, parents and guardians, community representatives, and other faculty. This does not mean that people outside the school have the right to censor a teacher's plan, but it does mean that parents or guardians and students should have the right *sans penalty* to not participate and to select an alternate activity.

Fourth, there is nothing wrong with students knowing your opinion about an issue as long as it is clear that the students may disagree without reprisal or academic penalty. However, it is probably best to wait and give your opinion only after the students have had full opportunity to study and report on facts and opinions from other sources. Sometimes it is helpful to assist students in separating facts from opinions on a particular issue by setting up on the overhead or writing board a fact-opinion table, with the issue stated at the top and then two parallel columns, one for facts, the other for related opinions.

A characteristic that has made this nation so great is the freedom for its entire people to speak out on issues. This freedom should never be stymied nor excluded from public school classrooms. Teachers and students should be encouraged to express their opinions about issues, to suspend judgment while collecting data, and then to form and accept each other's reasoned opinions. We must understand the difference between teaching truth, values, and morals and teaching *about* truth, values, and morals.

Children Must Be Protected from Dogma and Allowed Freedom to Learn and to Develop Their Personal Values and Opinions

As a public school teacher there are limits to your academic freedom, much greater than are the limits, for example, on a university professor. You must understand this fact. The primary difference is that the students with whom you work are not yet adults; as minors they must be protected from dogma and allowed the freedom to learn and to develop their values and opinions, free from coercion from those who have power and control over their learning.

DECISION MAKING AND LOCUS OF CONTROL: NO ONE KNOWLEDGEABLE EVER SAID THAT GOOD TEACHING IS EASY, BUT IT IS FUN AND INTRINSICALLY REWARDING

As teacher you may make a thousand or more nontrivial decisions every day. You will have made some decisions prior to meeting your students for instruction, others will be made during the instructional activities, and yet still others are made later as you reflect on the instruction for that day. Many of these decisions can and will affect the lives of students for years to come. You may see this as an awesome responsibility, which it is.

Coping Strategies: Avoiding Feelings of Aloneness

As a beginning teacher, you quickly become aware of the many responsibilities that rest on your shoulders and how alone you are when making the myriad of decisions each day. Unlike when you were a student teacher and were observed and given feedback about your teaching on a fairly regular basis, life for the first-year teacher can be very lonely, especially if there is no one to approach when you feel frustrated or troubled and burdened by this responsibility. Thus, you need to be proactive about identifying a supportive and person with whom you can vent, discuss, and explore your concerns. The first few months of the school year seem to be a particularly crucial time for the new teacher to have opportunity to discuss concerns with a mentor or other empathetic colleague.

While incompetent and burned out teachers simply become aloof to the students and to their professional commitment and responsibility, exemplary teachers discover more productive ways to cope, such as via personal reflection, deep breathing, mental and physical exercising, and temporarily getting away from school matters. For example, maintaining personal reflections in a journal, even if only a sentence fragment rather than a paragraph, weekly rather than daily, or as a daily e-mail sent to yourself, can help provide valuable insight and personal satisfaction regarding your professional growth. As reported elsewhere (May, 2001), one teacher keeps an apple-shaped book on her desk all year long to record the high points of her teaching: the day a student gave her an apple, the time one of her most difficult classes really got into a discussion on dreams, the time a struggling student became clearly engaged in learning.

I attribute my successful evolution as a teacher to three powerful instructional strategies:
- Respect for diversity
- Power of reciprocal learning
- Personal reflection

Theoni Soublis Smyth (2005)

Decision Making and Instruction

It is useful to consider instruction in terms of four rather distinct decision-making and thought-processing phases: the planning phase, the interactive phase, the reflective phase, and the projection phase (Costa, 1991). The planning phase consists of all those intellectual functions and decisions you will make prior to actual instruction. The interactive phase includes all the decisions made during the immediacy and spontaneity of the teaching act. Decisions made during this phase are likely to be more intuitive, unconscious, and routine than those made during the planning phase. The reflective phase is the time you will take to reflect on, analyze, and judge the decisions and behaviors that occurred during the teaching phase. As a result of this reflection, decisions are made to use what was learned in subsequent teaching actions. At this point, you are in the projective phase, abstracting from your reflection and projecting your analysis into subsequent teaching behaviors.

This May Be the First Job Where You Are Constantly Reflecting on Your Every Action

To continue working effectively at a challenging task (that is, to ease the stress of teaching) requires significant amounts of reflection. Writing reflections in a personal journal about your teaching and teaching experiences can be useful not only to ease the stress but also to improve your teaching. Sample reflective questions are: How did I feel about my teaching today? If I feel successful, what were the students saying and doing that made me feel that way? If I do not feel successful, what were the students saying and doing that made me feel this way? Would I do anything differently next time? If so, what and why? What changes to tomorrow's lesson need to be made as a result of today's?

It is while reflecting that you have a choice of whether to assume full responsibility for the instructional outcomes or whether to assume responsibility for only the positive outcomes and place blame for the negative outcomes on outside forces (e.g., parents and guardians or society in general, peers, other teachers, administrators, and textbooks and materials, or lack thereof). Where the responsibility for outcomes is placed is referred to as *locus of control*. Teachers who are intrinsically motivated and competent tend to assume full responsibility for the instructional outcomes, regardless of whether or not the outcomes are as intended from the planning phase. The beginning teacher can best assume this professional responsibility when there is a trusted, competent, and empathetic colleague or mentor with whom to regularly confer.

Retaining Creativity and Individuality While Teaching a Prescribed and Even Scripted Curriculum

Many school districts produce curriculum maps that incorporate state curriculum standards and the district's core of knowledge benchmarks. Teachers are held accountable for teaching these essential learnings, frequently in a specific sequence and time frame. Become very familiar with your school's curriculum expectations, preferably before students arrive for that first class meeting. Keep the standards in a location where you can quickly refer to them.

Some elementary school teachers in particular find themselves in a school where the curriculum in language arts or mathematics is highly scripted. If this is the situation for you, just remember that simply because the curriculum is scripted doesn't deny your own instructional planning and tweaking of the lessons for your unique group of children. Curriculum that is highly scripted is not necessarily antagonistic to student-centered and differentiated instruction. For example, after each daily lesson, with each student in mind, the lesson that follows will need tweaking by you. Regardless of the origin of a lesson, you, the teacher, will bring to the implementation of that lesson your own unique and creative self. Like in championship ice-skating, although others may plan the moves, the ultimate decisions, skill, and art of execution remain the ownership of individual skaters. Teachers who are most effective are those who have learned to modify the key variables of time, methodology, and grouping to help individual students achieve mastery of the key curriculum standards. For example, see Brighton (2002) for how one middle school social studies teacher balances differentiated instruction, best instructional practices, and state-mandated accountability.

DIFFERENTIATING THE INSTRUCTION: ENSURING THAT NO CHILD IS LEFT BEHIND

There is much about the nature of the school setting that, when allowed, can discourage any teacher from making efforts to individualize the instruction. Teachers often have from 25 to 35 or more students at any one time with whom to work. Often, these students are of the same age and may not be very different from one another in physical size. This is especially true with children in the primary grades. Moreover, tradition reinforces the notion that you are teaching a *group* rather than *individuals* who just happen to be grouped together. It is only when you begin to look at students individually that differences between and among them become apparent. To personalize the instruction, your challenge is to devise instructional methods that accommodate the individual variations in students in group settings.

Individualizing the instruction does not mean that you are to shunt each student off to work alone. As a matter of fact, individualized instruction can and most often does take place in dyads and small groups formed to meet specific needs of individual students. These pairs and small groups are usually temporary and flexible. There is no particular procedure or formula to recommend, except to say that you probably cannot individualize instruction if you teach your class as a whole group day after day. You need to make a careful study of individual students, their learning capacities, their strengths, and areas where they need to develop their skills and competencies.

Selected Strategies for Personalizing Instruction
Regardless of the number and diversity of students in your classroom, and regardless of their grade level or the subject matter, you can immediately provide an effective degree of differentiated instruction by using the following techniques.

- Begin study of a topic from where students are in terms of what they know (or think they know) and what they want to know about the topic. Strategies for doing this include K-W-L (see Figure 7, page 88) and "think-pair-share." For the latter, students are presented with a new concept or topic about to be studied, and in pairs they discuss what they already know or think they know about the topic. While the teacher records ideas on the board or overhead, pairs of students then share with the rest of the class what they know or think they know about the topic.
- Empower students with responsibility for decision-making, reflection, and self-assessment.

- Provide multiple instructional approaches (that is, using multilevel instruction in a variety of settings, from learning alone to whole-class instruction).

- Provide students with choices from a rich variety of pathways and hands-on experiences to learn more about the topic.

- Use interdisciplinary thematic instruction as often as is feasible.

DISCIPLINE: FEAR OF LOSING CLASSROOM CONTROL IS A MAJOR CONCERN OF MANY BEGINNING TEACHERS

Effective teaching requires a well-organized, businesslike classroom in which motivated students work diligently at their learning tasks, free from distractions and interruptions. Providing such a setting for learning is called *effective classroom management*.

Essential for effective classroom management is the establishment and maintenance of *classroom control*, that is, the process of controlling student behavior in the classroom. Classroom control involves both steps for preventing inappropriate student behavior (the *establishment aspect*) and ideas for responding to students whose behavior is inappropriate (the *maintenance aspect*).

In a well-managed classroom, students know what to do, have the materials needed to do it, and stay on task while doing it. The classroom atmosphere is supportive; the procedures for doing them are made clear and understood; the materials of instruction are current, interesting, and readily available; and the classroom proceedings proceed smoothly with few disruptions.

One can learn rather quickly the skills needed to effectively manage a classroom. Key to that effectiveness is your need to (a) plan lessons thoughtfully and thoroughly; (b) provide students with a pleasant, positive, and supportive atmosphere; (c) establish control procedures that are firmly and consistently applied; (d) prevent distractions, interruptions, and disturbances; and (e) deal quickly and unobtrusively with distractions and disturbances that are not preventable.

Beginning the School Year Well: Thorough Preparation Provides Confidence and Fosters Success

Beginning the school term well can make all the difference in the world. You should appear at the first class meeting (and every meeting thereafter) as well prepared and as confident as possible.

It is likely that every beginning teacher is to some degree nervous and apprehensive; the secret is to not appear to the students as nervous, hesitant, and anxious. Being well prepared goes a long way in providing the confidence necessary to cloud feelings of nervousness. Read on!

Preventing a Ship from Sinking Is Much Easier Than Saving a Sinking One: Errors to Avoid

During your first year of teaching, no one, including you, should expect you to be perfect. You should, however, be aware of common errors teachers make that often are the causes of student inattention and disruptive behaviors. It is probable that as much as 95 percent of classroom control problems are teacher-caused and preventable. In this section, you will find descriptions of errors commonly made by teachers. To have a most successful start to (and continuation of) your career, you will want to develop your skills to avoid making these errors. To avoid making these errors requires both knowledge of the potential errors and reflection upon one's own behaviors in relation to them.

As with all guidelines presented in this little book, the items are mostly age-level, grade-level, and subject matter neutral. My advice is to read each item and reflect on the personal significance each may have for you. Sometimes you may find it beneficial to discuss an item with a colleague.

1. *Inadequately attending to long-range and daily planning.* A teacher who inadequately plans ahead is heading for trouble. Inadequate long-term and sketchy daily planning is a precursor to ineffective teaching and, eventually, to teaching failure. Students are motivated best by teachers who clearly are working hard and intelligently for them.

2. *Emphasizing the negative.* Too many warnings to students for their inappropriate behavior—and too little recognition for their positive behaviors—do not help to establish the positive climate needed for the most effective learning to take place. Reminding students of procedures is more positive and will bring you quicker success than reprimanding them when they do not follow procedures.

Too often, teachers try to control students with negative language, such as "There should be no talking," "No gum or candy in class or else you will receive detention," and "No getting out of your seats without my permission." Teachers sometimes allow students, too, to use negative language with each other, such as "Shut up!" Negative language does not help instill a positive classroom environment. To encourage a positive classroom atmosphere, use concise, positive language. Tell students exactly what they are supposed to do rather than what they are not supposed to do. Do not allow the use of disrespectful and negative language in your classroom.

3. *Not requiring students to raise hands and be acknowledged before responding.* While ineffective teachers often are ones who are controlled by class events, competent teachers are in control of class events. You cannot be in control of events and your interactions with students if students are allowed to shout out their comments, responses, and questions whenever they have the urge. The most successful teacher is one who quickly establishes her or his control of classroom events.

In addition, indulging their natural impulsivity is not helping students to grow intellectually. As students develop impulse control, they more often think before acting. Students can be taught to think before acting or shouting out an answer. One of several reasons that teachers should usually insist on a show of student hands before a student is acknowledged and selected to respond or question is to discourage students from the impulsive, disruptive, and irritating behavior of shouting out in class. (Of course, certain groups of students, lessons, and small-group discussions, might proffer exceptions to this general rule.)

4. *Allowing students' hands to be raised too long.* When students have their hands raised for long periods of time before the teacher recognizes them and attends to their questions or responses, the teacher is providing them with time to fool around. Although you don't have to call on every student as soon as he or she raises a hand, you should acknowledge the student, such as with a nod or a hand signal, so the student can lower his or her hand and return to work. Then you should return to the student as quickly as possible. Your procedure for this should be clearly understood by the students and consistently practiced by you. This is but one specific example of a common error made by many beginning teachers in particular, that of not specifically planning, clearly communicating, and consistently applying procedures.

5. *Spending too much time with one student or one group and not monitoring the entire class.* Spending too much time with any one student or a small group of students is, in effect, ignoring the rest of the class. As a new teacher, it is unwise to ignore the rest of the class, even for a moment. Wise teachers practice their overlapping skill.

6. *Beginning a new activity before gaining the students' attention.* A teacher who consistently fails to insist that students follow procedures and who does not expect all students to be in compliance before starting a new activity is destined for major problems in classroom control. You must establish and maintain classroom procedures. Starting an activity before all students are in compliance is, in effect, telling the students that they don't have to follow expected procedures. You cannot afford to tell students one thing and then do another. In the classroom, your actions will always speak louder than your words. (See number 16.)

7. *Pacing teacher talk and learning activities too fast (or, in some instances, too slow).* Pacing of the learning activities is one of the more difficult skills for beginning teachers. Remember that students need time to disengage mentally and physically from one activity before engaging in the next. Such disengagement takes more time for a classroom of 30 or so students than it does for just one person, you. This is a reason that I advise that transitions (see page 90) be planned and written in your lesson plan.

8. *Using a voice level that is always either too loud or too soft.* A teacher's voice that is too loud day after day can become irritating to some students, just as one that cannot be heard or understood can become frustrating. If you think there might be a problem, ask a colleague to sit in on your class and give you feedback about your voice. Many persons have benefited from taking a speech communications class, prior to, during, or after becoming teachers.

9. *Assigning a journal entry without giving careful thought to the assigned topic.* If the topic or question about which students are supposed to write is ambiguous or obviously hurriedly prepared—that is, without your having given thought to how students will interpret and respond to it—students will judge that the task is mindless busywork (e.g., something for them to do while you take attendance), and on that they are absolutely correct. If they do it at all, it will be with a great deal of commotion and much less enthusiasm than were they writing on a topic that for them had meaning and importance.

10. *Standing too long in one place.* Most of the time in the classroom, the teacher should be mobile, schmoozing, "working the crowd." See number 11.

11. *Sitting while teaching.* Unless you are physically unable to stand or to do so for long periods of time, or you are teaching children of the early grades, in most situations as a beginning teacher there is no time to sit while teaching. It is difficult to monitor the group while seated. You cannot afford to appear that casual.

12. *Being too serious and not fun.* No doubt, good teaching is serious business. But students are motivated by and respond best to teachers who obviously enjoy working with them and helping them learn, and are sentient of their interests and lives.

13. *Falling into a rut by using the same teaching strategy or combination of strategies day after day.* This teacher's classroom will likely become boring, perhaps more so to older students. Because of the multitude of differences, students are motivated by and respond best to a variety of well-planned and meaningful learning activities.

14. *Inadequately using quiet wait time after asking a content question.* When expected to think deeply about a question, students need time to do that. A teacher who consistently gives insufficient time for students to think is teaching only superficially and at the lowest cognitive level and is destined for problems in student motivation and classroom control. If necessary, review and modify your use of questioning as an instructional tool. (For that see any of the three books by Kellough for years 2007 or 2008 listed at the end of this book.)

15. *Poorly or inefficiently using instructional tools.* The ineffective use of teaching tools such as questioning, the overhead projector, electronic media, and the writing board says to students that you are not a competent teacher. Would you want an auto mechanic who did not know how to use the tools of that trade to service your automobile? Would you want a surgeon who did not know how to use the tools of the trade to remove your tumor? Like a competent automobile mechanic or a competent surgeon, a competent teacher can select and effectively use the best tools available for the job to be done.

24

16. *Ineffectively using facial expressions and body language.* As discussed previously (number 6), your gestures and body language communicate more to students than your words do. For example, one teacher didn't understand why his class of seventh graders would not respond to his repeated expression of "I need your attention." In one 15-minute segment, he used that expression eight times. Studying video of that class period helped him understand the problem. His attire was very casual, and he stood most of the time with one hand in his pocket. At 5 foot, 8 inches, with a slight build, a rather deadpan facial expression, and an inexpressive voice, in the classroom he was not a commanding presence. Once he saw himself on video, he returned to class wearing a tie, and he began using his hands, face, and voice more expressively. It worked, making him a more effective teacher.

17. *Relying too much on teacher talk.* Beginning teachers in particular have a tendency to rely too much on teacher talk. Too much teacher talk can be deadly. Unable to discern between the important and the unimportant verbiage, students will quickly tune the teacher out.

Some teachers rely too much on verbal interaction techniques. Verbally reprimanding a student for his or her interruptions of class activities is reinforcing the very behavior you are trying to stop. In addition, verbally reprimanding a student in front of the student's peers may very likely backfire on you. Instead, develop your indirect, silent intervention techniques, such as eye contact, mobility, hand and facial gestures, silence, and body stance and proximity.

18. *Inefficiently using teacher time.* During the planning phase of instruction, think carefully about what you are going to be doing every minute of the instructional time, and then plan for the most efficient and therefore the most effective use of your time in the classroom. Consider the following example. A teacher is recording student contributions on a large sheet of butcher paper that has been taped to the wall. She solicits student responses, acknowledges those responses, holds and manipulates the writing pen, and writes on the paper. Each of those actions requires decisions and movements that consume valuable time and can distract her from the students. An effective alternative would be to have a reliable student helper do the writing while the teacher handles the solicitation and acknowledgment of student responses. The teacher then has fewer decisions and fewer actions to distract her. And she is less likely to lose eye contact and proximity with the students. Please read on!

19. *Talking to and interacting with only half the class.* While leading a class discussion, there is a tendency among beginning teachers to favor (by their eye contact and verbal interaction) only 40 to 65 percent of the students, sometimes completely ignoring the others for an entire class period. Feeling ignored, those students will, in time, become uninterested and perhaps unruly. Remember to spread your interactions and eye contact evenly. *Try to establish eye contact at least once each day with each student.* And when I say to "establish" eye contact, I mean that the student knows that you are looking at her or him. Of course, you need to be sensitive to a student from a culture where extended eye contact may be unwanted or less common.

20. *Collecting and returning student papers (or other materials) before assigning students something to do.* If, while turning in papers or waiting for their return, students have nothing else to do, they may get restless and inattentive. Establish a procedure for what students are expected to do during this transition when papers or other materials are being collected or returned. (See "Transitions During Lessons" on page 90.)

21. *Interrupting students when they are on task.* It is not always easy to get an entire class of young people on task. Once they are on task, don't you be a distracter. Try to give all instructions before students begin. Once on task, if there is an important point you wish to make, write it on the board. If you want to return papers while students are working, do it in a way and at a time that is least likely to distract them from their learning task.

22. *Using "shhh" to quiet students.* When doing that, the teacher tends to sound like a balloon with a slow leak, thus adding a distracting noise to the classroom. Do not use "shhh" in the classroom. If you are using it, delete it from your professional vocabulary before it becomes a habit.

23. *Using poor body positioning.* Develop your skill of withitness by practicing positioning your body so you can continue visually monitoring the entire class even while talking to and working with one student or a small group. Avoid turning your back for more than a second to even a portion of the class.

24. *Settling for less when you should be trying for more—not getting the most from student responses.* The most successful teachers expect and get the most from all their students. Don't hurry a class discussion; "milk" student responses for all you can, especially when discussing a topic that students are obviously interested in. Ask a student for clarification or reasons for his or her response. Ask for verification of data. Have another student paraphrase what a student said. Seek deeper thought and meaning. Too often, the teacher will ask a question, get an abbreviated—often one word and low cognitive level—response from a student, and then move on to new content. Instead, follow up a student's response to your question with a sequence of questions, prompting and cueing to elevate student thinking to higher levels of cognition.

25. *Using threats.* Avoid making threats of any kind. One teacher, for example, told her class that if they continued with their inappropriate talking, they would lose their break time. Rather than threatening the entire class of students, she should have had the consequence of loss of break time as part of the understood procedures and consequences and then taken away the break time for some students if warranted. A reminder of procedures and consequences is different than is the use of a threat. The difference between making a threat and that of reminding students of procedures and consequences is not minor. Read on!

26. *Punishing the entire class for the misbehavior of a few.* Although the rationale behind such action is clear (i.e., to get group pressure working for you), often the result is the opposite. Students who have been behaving well are alienated from the teacher because they feel they have been punished unfairly. Those students expect the teacher to handle the misbehaving students without punishing those who are not misbehaving, and they are right!

27. *Using global praise.* Global praise is nearly useless. An example is: "Class, your rough drafts were really wonderful." This is hollow and says nothing. It is simply another instance of useless verbalism from the teacher. Instead, be specific— tell what it was about their drafts that made them so wonderful. As another example, after a student's oral response to the class, rather than simply saying "Very good," tell what about the student's response was good. Or rather than saying to a child "I love your drawing," tell the student specifically what it is about the drawing that you love. Enough said?

28. *Using color meaninglessly.* The use of color on transparencies and the writing board, for example, is nice but will shortly lose its effectiveness unless the colors have meaning. If, for example, everything in the classroom is color-coded and students understand the meaning of the code, then using color can serve as an important mnemonic to student learning.

29. *Verbally reprimanding a student from across the classroom.* Not only is it a needless interruption of all students, by embarrassing the recipient student in the presence of his or her peers, it is likely to increase the "you versus them" syndrome, Reprimand, if necessary, but do so quietly and privately.

30. *Interacting with only a "chosen few" students rather than spreading interactions around to all.* As a beginning teacher, especially, it is easy to fall into a habit of interacting with only a few students, especially those who are most vocal. Your job, however, is to teach all students. To do that, you must be proactive, not merely reactive, in your interactions.

31. *Not intervening quickly enough during inappropriate student behavior.* When allowed to continue, inappropriate student behavior usually gets worse, not better. It's best to nip it in the bud quickly and resolutely. A teacher who ignores inappropriate behavior, even briefly, is, in effect, approving it. In turn, that approval reinforces the continuation and repetition of inappropriate behaviors.

32. *Not learning and using student names.* A teacher who does not know or use names when addressing students is viewed by the students as impersonal and uncaring. You should quickly learn their names and then refer to students by their names. Some teachers make an effort to learn some if not all their students' names before ever meeting them for the first time, usually by obtaining photographs before the first day of school.

33. *Reading student papers only for correct (or incorrect) answers and not for process and student thinking.* Reading student papers only for correct responses reinforces the false notion that the process of arriving at answers or solutions is unimportant and that alternative solutions or answers are impossible or unimportant. It negates the importance of the individual and the very nature of learning.

34. *Not posting time plans.* Yelling out how much time is left for an activity interrupts student thinking; it implies that to you, at least, their thinking is unimportant. Avoid interrupting students once they are on task. Show respect for their on-task behavior. In this instance, before the activity begins, post in a conspicuous place how much time is allowed for it. Highlight the time the activity is to end.

35. *Asking global questions that nobody likely will answer.* Examples are "Does everyone understand?" "Are there any questions?" and "How do you all feel about . . . ?" It is a brave young soul who, in the presence of peers, is willing to admit ignorance. It is a waste of valuable instructional time to make such queries. If you truly want to check for student understanding or opinions, then do a spot check by asking specific questions, allowing time to think, and then calling on students.

36. *Failing to do frequent comprehension checks (every few minutes during most direct instruction situations) to see if students understand.* Too often, teachers simply plow through a big chunk of the lesson, or the entire lesson, while only assuming that students understand. Or, in the worst-case scenario, teachers rush through a lesson without even seeming to care whether students are getting it. Students are quick to recognize teachers who don't care or don't seem to care.

37. *Not monitoring for understanding during seatwork.* Frequent comprehension checks should be done, too, when students are doing seatwork. When assigning seatwork, be sure that your instructions include specifics about what is to be learned, how it is to be learned, and how the content is connected to previous material. During seatwork, monitor students not only to keep them on task but also to check for individual understandings and to assist when necessary.

38. *Using poorly worded, ambiguous questions.* **Key** questions you will ask during a lesson should be thoughtfully planned and written into your lesson plan.

39. *Trying to talk over student noise.* This simply tells students that their making noise while you are talking is acceptable behavior. When this happens, everyone, teacher included, usually gets increasingly louder during the class period. About all that you will accomplish when trying to talk over a high student noise level is a sore throat by the end of the school day and, over a longer period of time, an increasing potential for nodules on your vocal cords.

Incidentally, because teachers experience voice problems much more frequently than do other workers, some school districts now are installing either portable (system is operated by the teacher) or infrared wireless voice enhancement systems. Such systems not only help teachers' vocal health but also increase student academic achievement (McCarty, Ostrem, & Young, 2004).

40. *Wanting to be liked by students.* Forget it. If you are a teacher, then teach. Respect is earned as a result of your effective teaching and professional demeanor. Liking you may come later. You are not your students' peer; you are their teacher—a professional and very important adult role model.

41. *Permitting students to be inattentive to an educationally useful media presentation.* This usually happens because the teacher has failed to give the students a written handout of questions or guidelines for what they should acquire from the program. Sometimes students need an additional focus. Furthermore, a media presentation is usually audio and visual. To reinforce student learning, add a kinesthetic component, such as the writing aspect.

42. *Starting in stutters.* A stutter start is when the teacher begins an activity, is distracted, begins again, is distracted again, tries again to start, and so on. During stutter starts, students become increasingly restless and inattentive, and sometimes even amused by the teacher's futility, making the final successful start almost impossible for the teacher to achieve. Avoid stutter starts. Begin an activity clearly and decisively. This is most easily accomplished when lesson plans are prepared thoughtfully and thoroughly. Also important to the prevention of stutter starts is the teacher's overlapping ability. For example, a teacher who can accept the admit slip of an incoming tardy student without missing a beat in the lecture being given by the teacher has developed overlapping skill. As another example, the teacher who can stop the ensuing inappropriate behavior of a student with the use of a nonverbal gesture without interrupting the content discussion or distracting the other students has overlapping skill.

43. *Introducing too many topics simultaneously.* It is important to not overload students' capacity to engage mentally by introducing different topics simultaneously. For example, during the first 10 minutes of class, a high school teacher started by introducing a warm-up activity, which was a writing activity with instructions clearly presented on the overhead. The teacher also verbally explained the activity, although she could have simply pointed to the screen, thereby nonverbally telling students to begin work on the writing activity (without disrupting the thinking of those who had already begun). A minute later the teacher was telling students about their quarter grades and how later in the period they would learn more about those grades. Then she returned to the warm-up activity, explaining it a second time (or a third time if one counts the detailed explanation already on the screen). Next she reminded students of the new tardy rules, thus introducing a third topic. At this time, however, most of the students were still thinking and talking about what she had said about quarter grades, few were working on the warm-up activity, and hardly any were listening to the teacher talking about the new tardy rules. There was a lot of commotion among the students; the teacher had tried to focus student attention on too many topics at once, thus accomplishing little and losing control of the class in the process.

29

44. *Failing to give students a pleasant greeting on Monday or following a holiday or to remind them to have a pleasant weekend or holiday.* Students are likely to perceive such a teacher as uncaring or impersonal.

45. *Sounding egocentric.* Whether you are or are not egocentric, you want to avoid appearing so. Sometimes the distinction is subtle, although apparent, such as when a teacher says, "What *I* am going to do now is . . ." rather than "What *we* are going to do now is . . . ." If you want to strive for group cohesiveness—a sense of "we-ness"—then teach not as if you are the leader and your students are the followers, but rather in a manner that empowers your students in their learning.

46. *Taking too much time to give verbal instructions for an activity.* Students become impatient and restless during long verbal instructions from the teacher. It is better to give brief instructions (60 seconds or less should do it) and get the students started on the task. For more complicated activities, teach three or four students the instructions for the activity and then have those students do workshops with five or six students in each workshop group. This frees you to monitor the progress of each group.

47. *Taking too much time for an activity.* No matter what the learning activity, think carefully about how much time students can effectively attend to the activity. A general guideline for most classes (age level and other factors dictate variation) is that when only one or two learning modalities are involved (e.g., auditory and visual), then the activity should not extend beyond about 15 minutes; when more than two modalities are involved (e.g., add tactile or kinesthetic), then the activity might extend longer, say for 20 to 30 minutes.

WHEN STUDENT ATTENTION BEGINS TO WANE

Today's youth are used to electronic interactions as well as "commercial breaks," and the capacity to surf channels to find something of interest to them. Thus, for many lessons, especially those that are teacher-centered, after about 8 minutes student attention is quite likely to begin to waft. For that eventuality you need lesson elements planned to recapture student attention. These planned elements can include:

- analogies to help connect the topic to students' experiences
- humor
- modality change such as from teacher talk to small-group work
- pauses for emphasis and to allow information to register
- sensory cues, such as eye contact and proximity (as is afforded by your moving around the room)
- verbal cues, such as voice inflections and name dropping
- visual cues, such as use of overhead displays, charts, board drawings, excerpts from CDs, realia, and body gestures

48. *Being uptight and anxious.* Consciously or unconsciously, students are quick to detect a teacher who is afraid that events will not go well. It's like a contagious disease; if you are uptight and anxious, your students will likely become the same. To prevent such emotions, at least to the extent they damage your teaching and students' learning, you must prepare lessons carefully, thoughtfully, and thoroughly. Unless there is something personal going on in your life that is making you anxious, you are more likely to be in control and confident in the classroom when your lessons are well prepared. How do you know when a lesson is well prepared? You will know! Usually, it's when you have developed a written lesson plan that you are truly excited about, proud of, and look forward to implementing.

If you do have a personal problem that is distracting you and making you anxious (and occasionally most of us do), you need to concentrate on ensuring that your anger, hostility, fear, or other negative emotions do not adversely affect your teaching and your interactions with students and colleagues. Regardless of your personal problems, your classes of students will face you each day expecting to be taught reading, mathematics, history, science, physical education, or whatever it is you are supposed to be helping them learn.

49. *Failing to apply the best of what we know about how young people learn.* Too many teachers unrealistically seem to expect success having all students in their classroom doing the same thing at the same time rather than having several alternative activities simultaneously occurring in the classroom, called *multilevel teaching*, or *multitasking*. For example, a student who is not responding well, who is perhaps being inattentive and disruptive to a class discussion, might behave better if given the choice of moving to a quiet reading center in the classroom or to a learning station to work alone. If, after trying an alternative activity, the student continues to be disruptive, then you may have to try still another alternative activity. You may have to send the student to another supervised location out of the classroom, to a place previously arranged by you, until you have time after class or after school to talk with the student about the situation.

50. *Overusing punishment for classroom misbehavior—jumping to the final step without trying intermediate alternatives.* Teachers sometimes mistakenly either ignore inappropriate student behavior (see number 31) or they skip steps for intervention, resorting too quickly to punishment. They immediately send the misbehaving student outside to stand in the hall (not a wise choice if the student is not supervised) or too quickly assign detention (a usually ineffective form of punishment). In-between steps to consider include the use of alternative activities in the classroom (as in number 49).

51. *Being inconcise and inconsistent.* Perhaps one of the most frequent causes of problems in classroom control for beginning teachers derives from when the teacher fails to say what is meant or mean what is said. A teacher who gives vague instructions and is inconsistent in his or her behaviors only confuses students (e.g., does not enforce his or her own classroom procedural expectations).

Helping Students Develop Self-Control

The best control is self-control. You can help your students develop self-control by (a) providing a rich and stimulating learning environment, (b) clearly and concisely expressing your expectations for student behavior and learning, (c) helping students establish a code of conduct for themselves, (d) helping students improve their own standards of conduct, (e) using a firm and consistent application of procedures and expectations, and (f) quickly and unobtrusively refocusing an inattentive student to an on-task behavior.

EQUALITY IN THE CLASSROOM: ENSURE A PSYCHOLOGICALLY SAFE AND SUPPORTIVE LEARNING ENVIRONMENT

When conducting class discussions, it is easy for a teacher to fall into the trap of interacting with only "the stars," or only those nearest the teacher, or only the most vocal and assertive. You must exercise caution and avoid falling into that trap. To ensure a psychologically safe and effective environment for learning for every person in your classroom, you must attend to all students and try to involve all students equally in all class activities. Otherwise, ignored students may feel discriminated against and become inattentive and even disruptive.

Examples of Teacher Behaviors That Violate the Concept of Gender Equity

Research has identified the unintentional tendency of teachers of *both* sexes to discriminate on the basis of gender. Some of the more common teacher behaviors that violate the concept of gender equity are these:

- Accepting unreservedly the assumption that females are less capable than males in such fields as mathematics, science, and athletics and, conversely, that males have less aptitude for art, literature, music, and dance.
- Administering harsher consequences to males than to females for the same rule infraction.
- Allowing boys to interrupt girls but praise girls for being polite and waiting their turn.
- Allowing or ignoring humor that ridicules one gender or the other, such as that directed toward the behavior of "nonmacho" males or women drivers.
- Consistently using generic terms such as *man, mankind, early man,* and *common man* when the reference is to humanity. It is better to substitute inclusive terms such as *people, human beings, ordinary people, humankind,* and *early people.*
- Displaying charts or graphs that compare the achievement of individuals according to gender.
- Exaggerating the emphasis on the socialization of children into traditional gender roles: neatness, conformity, docility, and fastidiousness for females;

32

competitiveness, aggressiveness, and physical activity and strength for males. It is important to maintain a balanced emphasis.

- Expressing a preference for teaching either males or females.
- Identifying certain leadership positions or specific activities in the classroom as being solely for one gender or the other.
- Interacting more with one gender than the other in class discussion.
- Making light of, ignoring, or even ridiculing social movements or individuals associated with movements to secure equity for women.
- Neglecting or ignoring the contributions of women to humankind in social studies, mathematics, and science, or wherever else it is relevant.
- Segregating children on the basis of gender, such as in the seating arrangement in the classroom, in playground games, and in classroom learning activities.

To avoid such discriminations may take special effort on your part, no matter how aware of the problem you may be.

Ensuring Equity

You must not discriminate against students on any basis for any reason! Guidelines that can help ensure that students are treated fairly in your classroom include the following:

- Avoid using gender-associated metaphors, such as "carry the ball" or "tackle the problem."
- Do your part to abolish practices that qualify as institutionalized racism, some of which are often so common and so subtle they go undetected. Examples are:
  1. Accepting implicitly the assumption that nonwhites are less capable than whites in any field of study or endeavor or, conversely, that nonwhites have specific aptitudes but are limited to those areas of achievement.
  2. Bias against the use of language other than English or against a child who speaks a dialect of English or with a non-English accent.
  3. Curriculum content unrelated to the life and culture of certain groups. This circumstance discriminates against those who are not represented in the subject matter of the school.
  4. Expectations that children of color are more likely to misbehave, combined with harsher and more frequent punishment for those children when they misbehave.
  5. Homogeneous grouping, a practice that discriminates against ethnic minorities because it often results in their being placed in low-achieving groups.
  6. Neglecting or ignoring the contributions of individuals of color to humankind in social studies, mathematics, and science, or wherever else it is relevant.
  7. References that portray black as bad and white as good.
  8. References that portray south as bad and north as good.

9. Social acceptance of a higher incidence of failure and a higher dropout rate among certain minorities.

10. Unnecessary and irrelevant references to an individual's or group's racial or ethnic identity, such as "the black mayor . . . ," "the Hispanic candidate from . . . ," "Asian parents gathered . . . ," or "the driver, an Indian from Hayfork, was charged with drunken driving." Such references are almost never used when the individual or group is white.

- During class instruction, insist that students raise their hands and be recognized and called upon by you before they speak out.

- Encourage students to demonstrate an appreciation for one another by applauding all individual and group presentations.

- Focus discussions on creative process thinking as often as on so-called correct answers.

- Insist on politeness in the classroom. Insist that students be allowed to finish what they are saying, without being interrupted by others. Be certain to model this behavior yourself.

- Keep a stopwatch handy to control unobtrusively the wait time given for each student. Although this idea may sound impractical, it can be used effectively.

- Maintain high expectations, although not necessarily identical expectations, for all students.

- Make a conscious effort to call on students equally for their responses and contributions in your classroom.

FIELD TRIP: PLANNING FOR SUCCESS

Today's schools often have very limited funds for the transportation and liability costs for field trips. In some cases, there are no funds at all, in which case student field trips are electronic, online only. At times, parent-teacher groups and business and civic organizations help by providing financial resources so that children get valuable first-hand experiences that off-campus field trips so often afford.

To prepare for and implement a successful field trip, there are three important stages of planning—before, during, and after—and critical decisions to be made at each stage. Consider the following guidelines.

Before the Field Trip

When the field trip is your idea (and not the students), discuss the idea with your teaching team, principal, or department chair (especially when transportation will be needed) *before* mentioning the idea to your students. Also you may discover that the place you had in mind is in fact an overused sight for field trips and that many or most of your students have already been there. Also carefully consider the worth of the proposed field trip; don't use valuable resources for field trips for trivial learnings.

The bottom line is that there is no cause served by getting students excited about a trip before you know if it is feasible.

Once you have obtained the necessary, but tentative, approval from school officials, take the trip yourself (or with team members), if possible. A previsit allows you to determine how to make the field trip most productive and what arrangements will be necessary. For this previsit you might consider taking a couple of your students along for their ideas and help. If a previsit is not possible, you still will need to arrange for travel directions; arrival and departure times; parking; briefing by the host, if there is one; storage of students' personal items, such as coats and lunches; provisions for eating and restrooms; and fees, if any.

If there are fees, you need to talk with your administration about who will pay the fees. If the trip is worth taking, the school should cover the costs. If that is not possible, perhaps students can plan a fund-raising activity or financial assistance can be obtained from some other source. If this does not work, you might consider an alternative that does not involve financial costs.

Arrange for official permission from the school administration. This usually requires a form for requesting, planning, and reporting field trips. After permission has been obtained, you can discuss the field trip with your students and arrange for permissions from their parents or guardians. You need to realize that although parents or guardians sign official permission forms allowing their children to participate in the trip, these only show that the parents or guardians are aware of what will take place and give their permission for their child to participate. Although the permission form should include a statement that the parent or guardian absolves the teacher and the school from liability should an accident occur, it does not lessen the teacher's and the school's responsibilities should there be negligence by a teacher, driver, or chaperone.

Arrange for students to be excused from their other classes while on the field trip. Using an information form prepared and signed by you and perhaps by the principal, the students should then assume responsibility for notifying their other teachers of the planned absence from classes and for assuring them that whatever work is missed will be made up. In addition, you will need to make arrangements for your own teaching duties to be covered. In some schools, teachers cooperate by filling in for those who will be gone. In other schools, substitute teachers are hired. Unfortunately, sometimes teachers must hire their own substitute.

Arrange to have a cell phone available for your use during the trip. Some schools have a cell phone available for just that purpose. If not, and you don't have your own, perhaps one of the drivers or other adult chaperones does have one. Check it out.

Arrange for whatever transportation is needed. Your principal, or the principal's designee, will help you with the details. In many schools, someone else is responsible for arranging transportation. In any case, for liability reasons the use of private automobiles is ill advised.

Arrange for collection of money needed for fees. If there are out-of-pocket costs to be paid by students, this information needs to be included on the permission form. No students should ever be excluded from the field trip because of a lack of money. This can be a tricky issue because there may be some students who would rather steal the money for a field trip than admit they don't have it. Try to anticipate problems;

hopefully the school or some organization can pay for the trip so that fees need not be collected from students and therefore potential problems of this sort are avoided.

Plan details for student safety and the monitoring of their safety from departure to return. Included should be a first-aid kit and a system of student control, such as a buddy system whereby students must remain paired throughout the trip. The pairs sometimes are given numbers that are recorded and kept by the teacher and the chaperones, and then checked at departure time, periodically during the trip, at the time of the return trip, and again upon return. Use adult chaperones. As a general rule, there should be one adult chaperone for every 10 students. Some districts have a policy regarding this. While on a field trip, at all times all students should be under the direct supervision of a dependable adult.

Plan the complete route and schedule, including any stops along the way. If transportation is being provided, you will need to discuss the plans with the provider. Establish and discuss, to the extent you believe necessary, the rules of behavior your students should follow. Included in this might be details of the trip, its purpose, directions, what they should wear and bring, academic expectations of them (for example, consider giving each student a study guide), and follow-up activities. Also included should be information about what to do if anything should go awry, for example, if a student is late for the departure or return, loses a personal possession along the way, gets lost, is injured, becomes sick, or misbehaves. For the latter, never send a misbehaving student back to school alone. Involve the adult chaperones in the previsit discussion. All of this information should also be included on the parental/guardian permission form.

If a field trip is supposed to promote some kind of learning (as undoubtedly will be the case, unless the sole purpose is something like an end of the term or end of unit celebration) then to avoid leaving it to chance, the learning expectations need to be clearly defined and the students given an explanation of how and where they may encounter the learning experience. Before the field trip, students should be asked questions such as, What do we already know about _____? What do we want to find out about _____? How can we find out? And then, with their assistance, an appropriate guide can be prepared for the students to use during the field trip.

To further ensure learning and individual student responsibility for that learning, you may want to assign different roles and responsibilities to students, just as would be done in cooperative learning, thus ensuring that each student has a role with responsibility.

You may want to take cameras or other recording equipment so the field-trip experience can be relived and shared upon return. If so, roles and responsibilities for the equipment and its care and use can be assigned to students as well.

During the Field Trip

If your field trip has been carefully planned according to the preceding guidelines, it should be a valuable and safe experience for all. Enroute, while at the trip location, and on the return to school, you and the adult chaperones should monitor student behavior and learning just as you do in the classroom.

After the Field Trip

Plan the follow-up activities. As with any other lesson plan, the field-trip lesson is complete only when there is both a proper introduction and a well-planned and executed closure. All sorts of follow-up activities can be planned as an educational wrap-up to this educational experience. For example, a committee can plan and prepare an attractive display summarizing the trip. Students can write about their experiences in their journals or as papers. Small groups can give oral reports to the class about what they did and learned. Their reports can then serve as springboards for further class discussion, and perhaps further investigations. Finally, for future planning, all who were involved should contribute to an assessment of the experience.

FIRST DAY: YOUR ONE OPPORTUNITY TO MAKE AN INITIAL IMPRESSION

I cannot exaggerate the importance of (a) the first day of school, (b) the first week of school, and (c) the first few minutes of each class meeting. For you, there will be just one opportunity to make a first impression on your students. The first few days of school set the tone for the entire year, and the first few minutes of each class meeting set the tone for the entire meeting.

On the first day, you will want to cover certain major points of common interest to you and your students. Consider the following.

Dress with Professional Pride
Dress for success. You are an adult and a professional; demonstrate pride in that fact. The correlation between your success as a teacher and your image as a professional is a direct one. Indeed, the correlation between how you perceive yourself and how others perceive you is a direct one. The cause of problems for some beginning teachers is due to their desire to be *liked* by their students, that is, to be accepted as a peer rather than perceived, admired, and respected as an adult role model and professional.

Greet the Students

Welcome the students with a smile as they arrive, and then greet the entire class with a friendly but professional demeanor. This means that you are not frowning, nor are you off in a corner of the room doing something else as students arrive. As you greet the students, tell them in a firm but pleasant voice (not too loud, not too hesitant or weak) to take a seat and start on the first assignment already on each desk. Keep the class moving along at a fairly rapid pace, with little to no dead time (i.e., time when students have nothing to do).

Initial Activity

After your greeting, begin the first meeting immediately with some sort of activity, preferably a written (or drawing) assignment already on each student desk. This assures that students have something to do immediately upon arriving to your classroom. That first activity might be a questionnaire each student completes. This is a good time to instruct students on the procedure for heading and turning in their papers.

Student Seating

One option is to have student names on the first assignment paper and placed at student seats when students arrive that first class meeting. That allows you to have a seating chart ready on the first day, from which you can quickly take attendance and learn student names. Another option, not exclusive of the first, is to tell students that by the end of the week each should be in a permanent seat (either assigned by you or student selected), from which you will make a seating chart so that you can quickly learn their names and efficiently take attendance each day. Let them know, too, that you will redo the seating arrangement from time to time (if that is true).

Information About the Class or Course

After the first assignment has been completed, discussed, and collected (allowing rehearsal of the procedure for turning in papers), explain to students about the class or course—what they will be learning and how they will learn it (covering study habits and your expectations regarding quantity and quality of work). Teachers of upper grades usually put this information in a course syllabus (see the sample in Figure 3), give each student a copy, and review it with them, specifically discussing the teacher's expectations about how books will be used; about student notebooks, journals, portfolios, and assignments; about what students need to bring from home; and about the location of resources in the classroom and elsewhere.

When creating a syllabus or organizing for instruction, it is advisable to seek guidance from your mentor or from a teacher who is recommended by the principal as a good role model.

Figure 3 Sample course syllabus (Courtesy of Angela Biletnikoff)

English 8   **Room 23, Mrs. Biletnikoff**

Course Description

English 8 is a course designed to provide instruction in the areas of reading, analyzing and writing about literature, while utilizing texts that support the coursework in History 8. Essay writing, especially descriptive writing, is emphasized. In addition to intensive vocabulary study, students will be writing on a daily basis. Also, the students will read one million words of outside texts, in addition to their assigned reading. The readings for English 8 are an eclectic mix (see the novels listed at the end of this syllabus).

Materials required

Students are required to bring pen, pencil, and paper to class each day. Journal binder should be a 2-pocket, 3-prong paper binder. The school provides the vocabulary text and all literary texts.

Goals

* To understand and recognize the various aspects of literature: character, setting, plot, point of view, and theme.
• To increase vocabulary, preparing students for more advanced writing.
• To develop and enhance students' descriptive writing and organizational skills.
• To increase oral and listening skills.

Objectives

• Students will participate in projects, class discussions, journal writing, quizzes, essay writing, and tests that are designed to help them grasp the concepts of plot, setting, character, theme, and other literary devices. Through these activities, students will demonstrate improvement in their writing and oral/listening skills.
• Students will participate in class activities such as sustained silent reading (SSR), read aloud, and project development to help in their learning of the material.

Assignments

There are weekly vocabulary quizzes. There is also weekly vocabulary homework. Throughout the course, students will be writing journal entries, quickwrites, and essays. All completed and graded work is returned to the corresponding class file. Students are free to check the file before or after class.

Assessment Components

• Students will complete weekly vocabulary quizzes.
• Quizzes are administered when the teacher needs to check the students' progress.
• Test dates will be announced in class and class time is used for test preparation.
• Students will complete weekly vocabulary quizzes.
• Quizzes are administered when the teacher needs to check the students' progress.
• Test dates will be announced in class and class time is used for test preparation.
• Class participation, including participation in group work, accounts for 15% of the student's grade; therefore, absences and tardiness can negatively affect this assessment component.

Method of Evaluation

Evaluation is done through oral and written quizzes and tests. Additionally, students are evaluated on class participation, assignments, projects, and class discussions. All grades are based on a point system.

Papers, quizzes, and tests	= 50% of total points
Homework	= 20% of total points
Journals	= 15% of total points
Group work and class participation	= 15% of total points

Grading Scale   90-100% of total points = A; 80-89% = B; 70-79% = C; 50-69% = D
< 50%= F; Grades are posted (by codes, not names) biweekly

Classroom Citizenship Behavior and Consequences for Inappropriate Behavior
Students are expected to demonstrate the 5Ps: be prompt, prepared, polite, productive, and positive
Students may earn 5 points per day by observing the 5Ps guidelines. Students may forfeit their citizenship points by excessive bathroom requests, tardiness, or leaving class without the teacher's approval.
Consequences for inappropriate behavior:
1st infraction = verbal warning
2nd infraction = 15 minutes at time out and a phone call to parent or guardian
3rd infraction = administrative referral and/or a call home
4th infraction = administrative referral and possible suspension
Note: any step in the above process may be skipped at the teacher's discretion.
Attendance
Regular attendance is crucial for success. It enables the student to understand assignments and to take advantage of the guidance provided by the teacher and others. In addition, the students will receive immediate feedback regarding their progress. If a student needs to leave early or enter late, please make arrangements with the teacher beforehand, if possible.
Tardiness
Students are tardy when they are not in their seats when the tardy bell rings. Any student who elects to leave the classroom for any reason takes a tardy for that period. Tardiness affects citizenship as well as the privilege to participate in extracurricular activities before and after school.
Bathroom Privileges
Students are allowed two bathroom passes per quarter. Each pass is redeemed at the time of use. If the student does not use the two passes for the quarter, the student receives 5 extra points per pass, with a total of 10 points possible towards their citizenship grade. If a student chooses to use the bathroom beyond the two-pass limit, then that student forfeits the citizenship points (5) for the day.
Make-up
Students may make up assignments one day after returning from an excused absence. All other work is accepted at the teacher's discretion.
Extra Credit Work There is no "extra credit" work in this class.
Instructional Schedule for English 8, Fall Semester
   Unit I   Introduction to the short story (2 weeks)
                 Vocabulary, journal, SSR, and outside readings begin
   Unit II   *April Morning* (4-5 weeks)
   Unit III *The Giver* (4-5 weeks)
   Unit IV *Diary of Anne Frank* (4-5 weeks)

Procedures and Endorsed Behavior

Now, while you are on a roll, discuss in a positive way your expectations regarding classroom behavior, procedures, and routines. Young people work best when teacher expectations are well understood, with established routines. In the beginning, it is important that there are no more procedures than are necessary to get the class moving effectively for daily operation. Five or fewer expectations should be enough, such as arrive promptly, remain on task until excused by the teacher, listen attentively, show mutual respect, use appropriate language, and demonstrate appreciation for the rights and property of others. Too many procedural expectations at first can be restricting and even confusing to students. Unless they are recent newcomers or children of early primary grades, most students already know these things, so you shouldn't have to spend much time on the topic, except for those items specific to your course, such as dress and safety expectations for laboratory courses, shop classes, and physical education. Don't be surprised or disappointed if the road at first is bumpy; finding and applying the proper level of control for a given group of students is a skill that you develop from experience. And, I might add, although the road will get smoother, it will never be completely free from the occasional rough spot.

Focus on Endorsed Attitudes and Behaviors

Although many schools traditionally have posted in the halls and in the classrooms a list of prohibited behaviors, exemplary schools and teachers focus on endorsed attitudes and behaviors. To encourage a constructive and supportive classroom environment, practice thinking in terms of "procedures" rather than of "rules," and of "consequences" rather than of "punishment." The reason is this: To many people, the term *rules* has a more negative connotation than does the term *procedures*. When working with a cohort of young people, some rules are necessary, but I believe using the term *procedures* has a more positive ring to it. For example, a classroom rule might be that when one person is talking, we do not interrupt that person until he or she is finished. When that rule is broken, rather than reminding students of the "rule," you can change the emphasis to a "procedure" simply by reminding the students, "What is our procedure (or expectation) when someone is talking?"

Once you have decided on your initial expectations, you are ready to explain them to your students and to begin rehearsing a few of the procedures on the very first day of class. Remember this: students work best in a positive atmosphere, when teacher expectations are clear to them; when procedures are stated in positive terms, are clearly understood and agreed upon, and have become routine; and when consequences for inappropriate behaviors are reasonable, clearly understood, and promptly and consistently administered.

What Students Need to Understand from the Start

As you prepare the expectations for endorsed classroom behavior, you need to consider some of the specifics about what students need to understand from the start. These specific points, then, should be reviewed and rehearsed with the students, sometimes several times, during the first week of school and then followed *consistently* throughout the school term. Important and specific things that students need to know from the start will vary considerably depending on whether you are working with first graders, high school seniors. or some level in-between, and whether you are teaching language arts, physical education, or a science laboratory or shop class. But generally each of the following paragraphs describes what all students need to understand from the beginning.

Signaling for Your Attention and Help. At least at the start of the school term, most teachers who are effective classroom managers expect their students to raise their hands until the teacher acknowledges (often by a nod) that the student's hand has been seen. With that acknowledgment, the student should lower his or her hand. The recommended procedure is that once you have acknowledged their signal, they are expected to return to their work.

As discussed earlier (on page 22, item 3 of "Preventing a Ship from Sinking"), expecting students to raise their hands before speaking allows you to control the noise and confusion level and to be proactive in deciding who speaks. The latter is important if you are to manage a classroom with equality—that is, with equal attention to individuals regardless of their gender, ethnicity, proximity to the teacher, or another personal characteristic. I am not talking here about students having to raise their hands before talking with their peers during group work; I am talking about disallowing students shouting across the room to get your attention and talking out freely and impulsively during whole-class instruction.

An important reason for expecting students to raise their hands and be recognized before speaking is to discourage impulsive outbursts. One of the instructional responsibilities shared by all teachers, regardless of grade level or subject, is to help students to recognize and develop intelligent behaviors. Learning to control impulsivity is one of the intelligent behaviors. Teaching children to control their impulsivity is a highly important responsibility that too often is neglected by too many teachers (and too many parents/guardians). To me, the ramifications of this are frightening.

To avoid student dependence on you and having too many students raising their hands for your attention, and to encourage positive interaction between and among the students, you may want to employ the "three before me" procedure. That is, if a student has a question or needs help, the student must quietly ask up to three peers before seeking help from you. As a beginning teacher, you need to try ideas and find what works best for you in your unique situation.

Entering and Leaving the Classroom. From the time that the class is scheduled to begin and until excused by the teacher, teachers who are effective classroom managers expect students to be in their assigned seats or at their assigned learning stations and to be attentive to the teacher or to the learning activity. This expectation works for college classes, for kindergarten, and for every level and class in-between. For example, students should be discouraged from meandering toward the classroom exit in anticipation of the passing bell or the designated passing time; otherwise, their meandering toward the door will begin earlier and earlier each day and the teacher will increasingly lose control. Besides, it is a waste of a very valuable and very limited resource—instructional time. From the very first day, the procedure should be that only you, not the clock or hall bell, dismiss students.

Maintaining, Obtaining, and Using Materials. Students need to know where, when, and how to store, retrieve, and care for items such as their coats, backpacks, books, pencils, and medicines; how to get papers and materials; and when to use the pencil sharpener and wastebasket. Classroom control is easiest to maintain when (a) items that students need for class activities and for their personal use are neatly arranged and located in places that require minimum foot traffic, (b) there are established procedures that students clearly understand, (c) there is minimum student off-task time, and (d) students do not have to line up for anything. Problems in classroom control will most certainly occur whenever some or all students have nothing to do, even if only briefly. Therefore, you should plan the room arrangement, equipment and materials storage, preparation of equipment and materials, and transitions between activities to avoid instructional delays and procedural confusion.

When Waiting Is Necessary. Although you should minimize time that students spend waiting, you may not be able to entirely eliminate it, such as when children must line up for return from recess or lunch, or at the drinking fountain. As a matter of fact, learning to wait is an intelligent behavior that can and should be learned. So part of your responsibility as a teacher includes helping children learn how to wait.

Leaving Class for a Personal Matter. Normally, students should be able to take care of the need for a drink of water or to go to the bathroom between classes; however, sometimes they do not, or for medical reasons or during long block classes they cannot. Reinforce the notion that they should do those things before coming into your classroom or during the scheduled times, but be flexible enough for the occasional student who has an immediate need. Follow established school procedures whenever you permit a student to leave class for a personal reason, which may, for reasons of personal safety, mean that students can leave the room only in pairs and with a hall pass or when accompanied by an adult.

Reacting to a Visitor or an Intercom Announcement. Unfortunately, class interruptions do occur, and in some schools they occur far too often and for reasons that are not as important as interrupting the teacher and students' learning would imply (see Figure 4 on page 44). For an important reason, the principal, vice-principal, or some other person from the school's office may interrupt the class to see the teacher or a student or to make an announcement to the entire class. Students need to understand what behavior is expected of them during those interruptions. When there is a visitor to the class, the expected procedure should be for students to continue their learning task unless directed otherwise by you.

Arriving Late to Class or Leaving Early. You must abide by school policies on early dismissals and late arrivals. Routinize your own procedures so students clearly understand what they are to do if they must leave your class early (e.g., for a medical appointment) or if they arrive late. Procedures should be such that the student's personal safety is never jeopardized, and that late arriving and early dismissal students do not disturb the learning in progress.

Figure 4: About class interruptions

It is disconcerting how often teachers and student learning in classrooms of some schools are interrupted by announcements from the intercom, telephone, or a visitor at the door. After all, no one would even consider interrupting a surgeon during the most climactic moments of an open-heart operation, nor a prosecuting attorney at the climax of her summation, but it seems far too often that teachers are interrupted, sometimes just at the moment they have their students at a critical point in a lesson. Once lost because of an interruption, student attention and that teachable moment are nearly impossible to recapture.

    School administrators and office personnel must sometimes be reminded that the most important thing going on in the school is that which teachers have been hired to do—teach. The act of teaching must be respected and not frivolously interrupted. In my opinion, except for absolutely critical reasons, teachers should never be interrupted after the first five minutes of a class period and before the last five minutes. That policy should be established and rigidly adhered to. Otherwise, after many years of being a student, the lesson learned is that the least important thing going on at the school is that which is occurring in the classroom. No wonder then it is so difficult for teachers in some schools to gain student attention and respect. That respect must be demonstrated starting from the school's central office.

    A second but equally important reason for such a rigid policy is that indeed if there is an emergency during this instructional period, everyone involved will understand that the reason for the ensuing classroom interruption is very serious.

Consequences for Inappropriate Behavior

Teachers who are effective classroom managers routinize their procedures for handling inappropriate behavior to ensure that students understand their responsibilities and the consequences for inappropriate behavior. Consequences are posted in the classroom.

    On the first day, you can point to the posted consequences and, depending on the age of your students and their language skills, simply remind students of the consequences or explain them in some detail. But don't spend an inordinate amount of time on the consequences; simply emphasize what they are and that they will be consistently enforced by you.

    Whether offenses subsequent to the first are those that occur on the same day or within a designated period of time, such as one week, is one of the many decisions you, members of your teaching team, department, or the entire faculty must make.

First Homework Assignment

End the first class meeting with a positive statement about being delighted to be working with the students, and then give the first homework assignment. Make this first homework assignment one that will not take too much student time and one that each student can achieve well with minimal effort. Be sure to allow yourself sufficient time to demonstrate where assignments will be regularly posted and to make assignment instructions clearly understood by every student, including a reminder of how you expect students to head and turn in their papers.

GUEST SPEAKER: MAKING IT A SUCCESSFUL LEARNING EXPERIENCE

Bringing outside speakers into your classroom can be, for students, a valuable educational experience, but not automatically so. In essence, guest speakers can be classified within a spectrum of four types, depending on their ability to inspire and inform. Unfortunately, if it is the first time you have used a particular guest speaker, then you may not know of which type the speaker will be. (1) Ideally, a speaker is both informative and inspiring. (2) A speaker may be inspiring but with nothing substantive to offer, except for the possible diversion it might offer from the usual rigors of classroom work. (3) A speaker might be informative but boring to students. (4) At the worst end of this spectrum is the guest speaker who is both boring and uninformative. The guest speaker who is of this fourth type should not be invited back.

To make sure that the experience is beneficial to student learning, consider the following guidelines.

- If at all possible, meet and talk with the guest speaker in advance to inform the speaker about your students and your expectations (learning objectives) for the presentation and to gauge how motivational and informative the speaker might be. If you believe the speaker might be informative but boring, then perhaps you can help structure the presentation in some way to make the presentation a bit more inspiring. For example, in cooperation with the speaker, plan to stop the speaker every few minutes and involve the students in questioning and discussions of points made.
- Prepare your students in advance with key points of information that you expect them to obtain.
- Prepare students with questions to ask the speaker, things the students want to find out, and information you want them to inquire about.
- Follow up the presentation with a thank you letter to the speaker and perhaps additional questions that developed during class discussions following the speaker's presentation.

HIGH-ENERGY DAYS AND THE DISRUPTION OF ROUTINE: KIDS ARE HUMAN, TOO

It is helpful to be aware of your moods and days of high stress, that is, to anticipate that your tolerance levels may vary. It helps to let your students know when your mind may be elsewhere or when your tolerance for foolishness may be at a lower than normal level.

Young people, too, have days of high stress and anxiety. As you come to know your students, you will be better able to tell when certain students are experiencing an unusual amount of stress and anxiety, times when they may need extra listening and understanding. Many children come to school with so much psychological baggage that it is a wonder they come at all and that they can concentrate on schoolwork when they do.

Understand that there are perfectly natural reasons why classroom routines are likely to be interrupted occasionally, especially on certain days and at certain times during the school year. Students will not have the same motivation and energy level on each and every day. Energy levels may also vary throughout the school day. Your anticipation of—and thoughtful and carefully planning for—periods of high or low energy levels are important to your professional success and personal well-being. Depending on a number of factors, including the age level and school, periods of high energy level might include the following:

- At the beginning of each school day
- Before a field trip, a holiday, or a school event
- On a holiday (such as Valentine's Day or Halloween)
- On days of major testing
- On the day following a holiday
- On a grade report day
- Immediately before lunch and after lunch
- On a minimum day or the day a substitute teacher is present
- On the day of the year's first snowfall
- On the first warm day after a long cold period
- Toward the end of each school day
- Toward the end of school each Friday afternoon
- Toward the end of the school year

Additionally, although there may be no hard evidence, many veteran teachers affirm that particularly troublesome days for classroom control are those days when there is a strong north wind or a full moon. One teacher jokingly (I suspect) said on days when there is both a strong north wind and a full moon, she calls in sick.

What guidelines will help you prepare for these so-called high-energy days? There are probably no specific guidelines that will work for all teachers in all situations and in each instance from the list. However, these are days to which you need to pay extra attention during your planning. Students could possibly be restless and more difficult to control on these days, and you may need to be especially forceful and consistent in your enforcement of procedures or even compassionate and more tolerant than usual. Plan instructional activities that might be more readily accepted by the students. Never, however, do I mean to imply that learning ceases and playtime takes over. What little instructional time is available to a teacher is too valuable for that to happen.

46

HIGH-STAKES TESTING: CHECKING THAT NO STUDENT IS LEFT BEHIND

The adoption of tougher K-12 learning standards throughout the United States, coupled with an emphasis on increased high-stakes testing to assess how schools and teachers are doing with respect to helping all students meet those standards, has provoked considerable debate, actions, and reactions among educators, parents, and politicians, and from the world of business. Some argue that this emphasis on testing means too much "teaching to the test" at the expense of more meaningful learning, that it ignores the leverage that home, community, and larger societal influences have over the education of young people today. Nevertheless, responding to the call for increased accountability, for leaving no child behind, especially (although certainly not exclusively) when state and federal funding may be withheld and/or jobs are on the line for schools, teachers, and administrators where students do not score well, teachers have found various ways of working in the current culture of high-stakes testing. In some schools, teachers put aside the regular curriculum for several weeks in advance of the testing date and concentrate on the direct preparation of their students for the test. In some classrooms, preparing students for testing is a focal point of daily instructional practice. In short, educators are working at finding out what is best in their situations. As a new teacher, you will be expected to participate in this endless search for the best education for each student.

Differentiating Your Classroom: Modify the Key Variables of Time, Methodology, and Grouping

No one truly knowledgeable about it ever said that each student in your classroom should be learning the same thing, in the same way, at the same time. Effective teachers collect data on almost a daily basis on individual students and, from those data, make modifications in what each student should be learning, how they will learn it, and how they will demonstrate their learning. To differentiate and individualize the learning, on any given day you will use a variety of strategies—various sorts of learning groups, project-based learning, personalized learning plans, independent study, and mentoring.

INTERNET: VALUABLE RESOURCE TO ENHANCE TEACHING AND STUDENT LEARNING

Originating from a U.S. Department of Defense project in 1969 (called ARPAnet) to establish a computer network of military researchers, its successor, the federally funded Internet, has become an enormous, steadily expanding, worldwide system of connected computer networks. Because new technologies are steadily emerging and because the Internet changes every day, with some sites and resources disappearing or not kept current, with others having changed their location and undergone reconstruction, and with new ones appearing, it would be superfluous for me to make too much of sites that I have found and can recommend as teacher resources.

Nevertheless, Figures 5 and 6 (on pages 66-68) are listings of Internet sites that I have surfed and can recommend as resources to enhance your teaching.

Figure 5: Sample Internet resources for teachers

Beginning Teacher's Tool Box **http://www.inspiringteachers.com**
• *Council of the Great City Schools* **http://cgcs.org**, descriptions of programs and projects in urban schools
• *EdIndex* **http://www.pitt.edu/~poole**
• *EDSITEment* **http://www.edsitement.neh.gov** for humanities web sites
• *Education World* **http://www.education-world.com**, electronic version of *Education Week*
• *Educator's Reference Desk* **http://www.eduref.org**, to search ERIC Database
• *ENC* **http://www.enc.org**, Eisenhower National Clearinghouse for Mathematics and Science Education; resources, activity guides, links to schools
• Encyclopedia Mythica **http://www.pantheon.org/mythica/**, mythology, folklore, and legends
• *FedWorld* **http://www.fedworld.gov**, subject index to U.S. government; access to information from government agencies and departments
• *GEM, the Gateway to Educational Materials* **http://www.thegateway.org**
• *Global Schoolnet Foundation* **http://www.gsn.org/**, for resources and links for parents, teachers, and students from around the world
• *I Love Teaching* **http://www.iloveteaching.com**
• Instructional technology clearinghouse **http://clearinghouse.k12.ca.us**
• *Learn the 'Net* **http://www.learnthenet.com**
• *Library of Congress* **http://lcweb.loc.gov/homepage/lchp.html**
• *MainFunction Sources for Education* **http://www.mainfunction.com**, Microsoft's web site for distance learning and computer programming
• *MiddleWeb* **http://www.middleweb.com**, middle school focus
• *Newspapers in Education* **http://ole.net/ole/**
• *PedagoNet* **http://www.pedagonet.com**, learning resources database
• *School Match* **http://schoolmatch.com**, directory of schools
• Teacher's exchanges: **http://www.pacificnet.net/~mandel/**; **http://www.teachnet.org**; **http://www.teachersfirst.com**; and **http://www.kidinfo.com**
• *United Nations' CyberSchool Bus* **http://www.un.org/Pubs/CyberSchoolBus/**
• *United States Copyright Office* **http://lcweb.loc.gov/copyright**
• *United States Department of Education* **http://www.ed.gov/index.html**
• WWW4Teachers **http://4teachers.org**

JOB SATISFACTION: A TWO-WAY STREET

There is no question that when, in the United States, so many new teachers drop out of the profession during the first five years, improving job satisfaction for teachers is paramount. New teacher induction programs are designed to help retain the best new teachers.

You have invested time and money in getting this far on your professional journey; it is important you do everything you can to find the satisfaction necessary to continue to grow toward becoming the best teacher you can be. Following the guidelines offered in this book is one step toward that becoming.

MAKEUP WORK: BE FIRM BUT UNDERSTANDING

Students at times will be absent and will miss assignments and tests, so it is best that your policies about late assignments and missed tests be clearly communicated to students and to their parents or guardians. Consider the following.

Homework Assignments

Although homework for students can be valuable and useful to their learning, it must be sensible, reasonable, and meaningful, or else it only alienates students (and parents/guardians). For example, there is no educational sense at all in all students doing identical assignments. There is no educational sense in assigning 20 problems to be done by a student who already knows full well how to do it. And, in too many instances, the school's treatment for students identified as being gifted is simply to overload them with homework. For the greatest success, in the time that you have, try to personalize homework assignments. Regardless of anything else, avoid giving students what only amounts to meaningless busywork. Before giving any assignment to students, ask yourself how you would feel were you given the assignment to do.

Late Work and Opportunity for Recovery

As a general policy, after due dates have been negotiated or set for assignments, give only reduced credit or no credit for work that is turned in late. Sometimes, though, a student has a legitimate reason why he or she could not get an assignment done by the due date, and for each instance you must exercise professional judgment. (Consider the classroom vignette "Late Homework Paper from an At-Risk Student.") Although it is important that you have established policies—and that you are fair in your application of those policies—you are a professional who should consider all aspects of a student's situation and, after doing so, show compassion for the human situation. As is often said, there is nothing democratic about treating unequals as equals. It is my opinion that the teacher should listen and exercise professional judgment in each instance.

Although it is important to encourage high quality and timely initial efforts by students, sometimes, for a multitude of reasons, a student's first effort is inadequate or

49

is lacking entirely. Perhaps the student is absent from school without legitimate excuse, or the student does poorly on an assignment or fails to turn in an assignment on time, or at all. Although accepting late work from students is extra work for the teacher, and although allowing the resubmission of a marked or tentatively graded paper increases the amount of paperwork, I believe it is worthwhile to give students opportunity for recovery and a limited time to make corrections and resubmit an assignment for an improved score. However, out of regard for students who do well from the start and meet initial due dates, it is probably ill advised to allow a late or resubmitted paper to receive an A grade.

TEACHING IN PRACTICE

Late Homework from an At-Risk Student

An eleventh-grade student turned in an English class assignment several days late and the teacher, without penalty, accepted the paper, although the teacher's policy was that late papers would be severely penalized. During the week that the assignment was due, the student had suffered a miscarriage. In this instance, her teacher accepted the paper late sans penalty because the student carried a great deal of psychological baggage and the teacher felt that turning in the paper at all was a positive act; if the paper had not been accepted, or had been accepted only with severe penalty to her grade, then, in the teacher's opinion, the student would have simply quit trying and probably dropped out of school altogether.

Tests and Quizzes

When students are absent during testing, you have several options, such as the following.

- Allow the student to miss or discount one test per grading period.
- Allow the student to substitute a written homework assignment or project for one missed test.
- Give the student the choice of either taking a makeup test or having the next test count double. When makeup tests are given, the makeup test should be taken within a week of the regular test unless there is a compelling reason (e.g., medical or family problem) why this cannot happen.

Sometimes students miss a testing period, not because of being absent from school, but because of involvement in other school activities. In those instances, the student may be able to arrange to take the test during another of your class periods, or your prep period, on that day or the next. If a student is absent during performance testing, the logistics and possible diminished reliability of having to re-administer the test for one student may necessitate giving the student an alternate paper-and-pencil test or some other option.

Many teachers give frequent and brief quizzes, as often as every day. As opposed to tests, quizzes are usually brief (perhaps taking only five minutes of class time) and intended to reinforce the importance of frequent study and review. When quizzes are given at frequent intervals, no single quiz should count very much toward the student's final grade. Therefore, you will probably want to avoid having to schedule and give makeup quizzes. The following are reasonable options to administering makeup quizzes and are presented here in order of my preference, beginning with my first choice:

1. Give a certain number of quizzes during a grading period, say, ten, but allow a student to discount a few quiz scores, say, two of the ten, thereby allowing the student to discount a low score or a missed quiz due to absence or both.

2. Count the next quiz double for a student who missed one due to absence. About the only problem with this option is when a student misses several quizzes in a row. If that happens, then try option three.

3. Count the unit test a certain and relative percentage greater for any student who missed one or more quizzes during that unit of instruction.

Unannounced Quizzes

When given and used for grades, "pop" or unannounced quizzes serve no useful educational purpose. They only alienate students. My advice: use them for review but *not* for grading purposes.

MEDIA: IF ANYTHING CAN GO WRONG, IT PROBABLY WILL!

When using media, it is nearly always best to set up the equipment and have it ready to go before students arrive. That helps avoid problems in classroom management that can occur when there is a delay because the equipment is not ready. After all, if you were a surgeon ready to begin an operation and your tools and equipment weren't ready, your patient's life would likely be placed in jeopardy. Like any other competent professional, a competent teacher is ready when the work is to begin.

Of course, delays may be unavoidable when equipment breaks down. Remember Murphy's law, which says that if anything can go wrong, it will. It is particularly relevant when using media equipment. You want to be prepared for such emergencies. Effectively planning for and responding to this eventuality is a part of your system of classroom management and takes place during the planning for your instruction. That preparation includes consideration of the following.

When equipment malfunctions, keep in mind three principles: (1) avoid dead time for students in the classroom, (2) avoid causing permanent damage to equipment, and (3) avoid losing content continuity of a lesson. So what do you do when equipment breaks down? Again, the answer is to be prepared for the eventuality.

Be Prepared with Plan B

If during brain surgery, a patient's brain artery suddenly and unexpectedly breaks, the surgeon and other members of the surgical team are ready for that eventuality and make the necessary repair. If while working on an automobile, a part breaks, the mechanic substitutes a replacement part. If while teaching, a computer program freezes or aborts on the screen or if a fuse blows or for some other reason you lose power and you feel that there is going to be too much dead time before the equipment is working again, that is the time to go to an alternate lesson plan. You have probably heard the expression "Go to Plan B." It is a useful phrase; what it means is that without missing a beat in the lesson, to accomplish the same instructional objective or another objective, you immediately and smoothly switch to an alternate learning activity. For you, an already overloaded beginning teacher, it doesn't mean that you must plan two lessons for every one, but that when planning a lesson that utilizes media, you should plan in your lesson an alternative activity, just in case. Then, if necessary, you move your students into the planned alternative activity quickly and smoothly.

MEMORIZING: SOMETIMES IT'S NECESSARY

There are times when students must memorize. There is even a time for memorization without much understanding. For example, to learn a language, you must first memorize the alphabet. To learn to play the clarinet, you must memorize the fingering. To learn mathematics, you must first memorize the numbering system. In the study of chemistry, you memorize the symbols for the elements. The alphabet, the fingering on the clarinet, numbers, and symbols are all kinds of tools. In mathematics certain assumptions must be memorized before other concepts can be developed. In fact, in all discipline, there are basic points that must be memorized before a learner can understand the major concepts.

When teaching through memorizing, the following guidelines are helpful:

- *Avoid overuse of memorizing.* Be sure there is a purpose for the memorizing and that the students understand what that purpose is.

- *If possible, have students study for meaning before memorizing.* Some things must be memorized, meaningful or not, such as German word order or Mandarin letters, whose shapes may seem arbitrary. These are tools of the trade, and they must be mastered to move on. But it is much easier to memorize those things that have meaning if you understand the meaning.

- *Encourage the use of mnemonics to aid students in their organization and memorization*—devices students invent or ones supplied by you. Mnemonics increase not only short-term recall but also increase long-term remembering. Examples of common mnemonic devices are: The notes on a treble staff are *FACE* for the space notes and *E*mpty *G*arbage *B*efore *D*ad *F*lips (*EGBDF*) for the line notes. The notes on the bass staff are *A*ll *C*ows *E*at *G*ranola *B*ars or *G*rizzly *B*ears

Don't *F*ly *A*irplanes (GBDFA). The names of the Great Lakes: HOMES for *H*uron, *O*ntario, *M*ichigan, *E*rie, and *S*uperior. Visual mnemonics are useful too, such as remembering that Italy is in the shape of a boot.

- Enjoyable games can help students with memorizing.

TEACHING IN PRACTICE

Games in the Classroom and the Underperforming Student

High-stakes state assessments have recently spotlighted the underperforming student. Faced with the probability of barring a large number of students from graduation, one high school teacher found a unique way to get students excited about studying the language arts and math skills required for the state tests.

The teacher, while at Camelback High School (Phoenix, AZ), was assigned to teach a special class for those students who were likely to fail the state graduation test. The students, including a good number of special-needs and students still learning English, were generally apathetic toward trying again to learn what they had failed to learn in math and English class.

They were apathetic, that is, until their teacher told them, "Put away your pencils and notebooks. Today we're going to play a video game!" After a demonstration by the teacher of how the game worked, the students, every single one of them, were concentrating hard on achieving the best score in the class . . . on a video game. In a few minutes Jacinto, one of the more competitive students, exclaimed, "I beat the game." The teacher recorded Jacinto's score and encouraged Jacinto to try to beat the game in fewer than 100 seconds. Jacinto accepted the challenge.

Did the students know that they were learning math? Certainly. The goal of the game was to state the range and domain (e.g., $22 < y < 97$ and $x < 144$) of ten randomly displayed functions. Once a student earned an A for beating the game, that student was encouraged to earn another A by turning in a time of under 100 seconds. Toward the end of the period, Jacinto and four other students were vying for the lowest time. When the dismissal bell rang, Ana had beaten Jacinto by 1 second, but the real reward was when they were asked to express the range and domain of a function on the state math assessment test.

Source: Courtesy of Mark Greenberg, now an English teacher at Phoenix Union Cyber High School (Phoenix, AZ).

MOTIVATIONAL IDEAS: BUILD YOUR REPERTOIRE

Today's youth are used to multimillion-dollar productions on television, DVDs, arcade games, and the movie screen. When they come into a classroom each day and are subjected to something short of a high-budget production, it is little wonder that they sometimes react in a less than highly motivated fashion. No doubt, children today are growing up in a highly stimulated, instant-action society, a society that has learned to expect instant headache relief; instant meals; instant gratification; instant communication; and perhaps, in the minds of many young people, instant high-paying employment. In light of this cultural phenomenon, I am on your side. As classroom teacher you are on the firing line for six hours a day, five days a week, and are expected to perform, perhaps instantly and entertainingly, in a highly competent and professional manner, and in situations not even close to ideal. In any case, you must capture students' attention before you can teach them.

The following is an annotated list of ideas for capturing student attention; see Figure 5 for additional Internet sources. Although the ideas are organized according to subject fields and may or may not be appropriate for all students and grade levels, *I suggest you read all entries for each field.* Although one entry might be identified as specific to a particular field, it might also be useful in other areas. Or it might stimulate a creative thought for your own stock of motivational techniques, such as an idea for a way to utilize the theory of multiple learning capacities or to emphasize the multicultural aspect of a lesson in math, social studies, or whatever the central discipline or theme of a lesson or unit of instruction.

The Visual and Performing Arts

1. As part of a unit combining design or creativity with science, have students construct, design, and decorate their own kites. Designate a time to fly them.

2. Use lyrics from popular music to influence class work, such as putting the lyrics into pictures.

3. Utilize the outdoors or another environment for a free drawing experience.

4. Invite a local artist who has created a community mural to speak to the class about the mural. Plan and create a class mural, perhaps on a large sheet of plywood or some other location approved by the school administration. For example, for several years at Chartiers Valley Intermediate School (Pittsburgh, PA), as a culminating project, each fifth grade class has contributed its own section to a growing mural in the school cafeteria.

   a. In another example, students in a rural Missouri high school collaborated online with students in an urban New York high school to create a mural in real space that celebrates the strengths of their two communities (Stein, 2001).

5. Create a mandala to demonstrate the importance of individual experience, as in interpreting paintings and poetry.

6. Study masks. Collect various media sources that show masks worn by people from around the world. Ask students to identify the similarities and differences in the masks. Have them research the meanings that mask characters have in various cultures. Have students design and create their own masks to illustrate their own personalities, cultures, and individualities.

54

7. As a portion of a unit on the creative process, have each student draw or sketch on a piece of paper, then pass it on to the next person, and that person will make additions to the drawing. Instructions could include "improve the drawing," "make the drawing ugly," "make the drawing seventeenth century," and "add what you think would be necessary to complete the composition."

8. Instructions for students: Imagine that you're a bird flying over the largest city you have visited. What do you see, hear, smell, feel, and taste? Draw a "sensory" map.

9. Assign a different color to each student. Have the students arrange themselves into warm and cool colors and explain their decisions (why blue is cool, etc.). Discuss people's emotional responses to each of the colors.

10. Watch video of dances from various countries and cultures. Invite students to identify similarities and differences. Ask them to research the meanings and occasions of particular dances.

11. Challenge students to discover ways in which music, art, and dance are used in their community.

12. Find a popular song that students like. Transpose the melody into unfamiliar keys for each instrument. This makes the student want to learn the song, but in the process the student will have to become more familiar with his or her instrument.

13. Set aside one weekend morning a month and hold small, informal recitals (workshops) allowing students to participate/observe the performance situation(s) among their peers and themselves. (Students might be told previously about these "special days" and encouraged to prepare a selection of their own choosing.)

14. Play a group-activity rhythm game, such as the "Dutch Shoe Game," to get students to cooperate, work together, and enjoy themselves using rhythm. Participants sit in a circle, and as the song is sung, each person passes one of his or her shoes to the person on the right in rhythm to the music. Shoes continue to be passed as long as verses are sung.

15. Choose a rhythmical, humorous poem or verse to conduct as if it were a musical work. The students read the poem in chorus while you stand before them and conduct. Students must be sensitive to the intonation, speed, inflection, mood, and dynamics that you expect them to convey in their reading.

16. Organize a Retired Senior Citizens Volunteer Program (RSCVP) with senior citizens presenting folk art workshops with students, and where the students and seniors work together to create artwork for the school and community.

17. Have students organize an Improv Troupe that creates and performs unscripted, improvisational skits about social issues relevant to today's youth.

Family and Consumer Economics, Foods, and Textiles

18. Often the foods we like originated from another area of our country or another place in the world. Have your students identify such foods and from where they

55

came—foods such as spaghetti, enchiladas, fajitas, wontons, tacos, quiches, croissants, teriyaki, fried rice, pizza, hot dogs, hamburgers, noodles, tomatoes, chocolate, potatoes, hoagies, chop suey, ice cream cones, submarines, and poor boys. Have them list the names and origins, and place pictures of the food in place on a large world map.

19. Take photos of class members at special events such as dinners, fashion shows, field trips, and projects. Build a scrapbook or bulletin board with these and display on campus or on the school web site and at spring open house or in a hallway display case.

20. Plan thematic units on cultural foods, using the traditions, costumes, and music of a particular culture. Have students decorate the room and invite the principal, school board president, and city mayor for a visit and perhaps a tasting treat.

21. Have a committee of students plan and create a school hallway display of pictures of 100-calorie portions of basic nutritional foods and popular fad foods that contain only empty calories. Do the same with pictures of foods and their specific carbohydrate contents.

22. Pin the names of different garments on the backs of students. The students are then challenged to sort themselves into different wash loads.

23. Organize a "new look day." Ask each student to bring in an idea of something that can be done to give clothes a new look, a fun touch, or an extended wearing life. Their ideas may include appliqués, embroidery, tie-dye, batik, colorful patches, and restyling old clothes into current or creative fashions.

24. Have the students research, create, write, practice, and present skits on consumer fraud and on identity theft.

25. Once a month, have students plan a menu, prepare the food, and serve it to invited senior citizens from the community.

26. Organize a program with senior citizens and students working together on a community garden.

27. Plan a program at a senior citizens' center whereby students and seniors work together on planning and decorating the center for special occasions and holidays.

28. With your students, plan a community service program. For example, at Discovery Middle School (Vancouver, WA), students provide childcare, cross-age tutoring, and companionship to preschool, elementary school, and elderly clients at off-campus locations.

29. Have students work on a project about culture and how culture affects our lives, such as the way we dress, eat, worship, socialize, celebrate, and communicate.

30. Challenge students to plan ways to educate the school and surrounding community about general nutrition and exercise.

English, Languages, and the Language Arts

31. Organize a paper or electronic letter-writing activity between senior citizens and your students.

32. For a unit on the Renaissance, have students create a wall-to-wall mural depicting a village of the times. Teams of students can research customs, costumes, and architecture. Others may paint or draw.

33. On a state or U.S. road map, have students find the names of places that sound "foreign" and categorize the names according to nationality or culture. Students could research when and how places got their names.

34. Set up this problem to enhance understanding of parts of speech. Provide several boxes (shoe boxes work fine) containing different parts of speech. Each student is to form one sentence from the fragments chosen from each box, being allowed to discard only at a penalty. The students then nonverbally make trades with other students to make coherent and perhaps meaningfully amusing sentences. A student may trade a noun for a verb but will have to keep in mind what parts of speech are essential for a sentence. Results may be read aloud as a culmination to this activity.

35. Students can match American English and British English words (or any other combination of languages), such as cookies and biscuits, hood and bonnet, canned meat and tinned meat, elevator and lift, flashlight and torch, subway and tube, garbage collector and dustman, undershirt and vest, sweater and jumper, and gasoline and petrol. Have students compare pronunciations and spellings.

36. English words derive from many other languages. Have students research and list some, such as ketchup (Malay), alcohol (Arabic), kindergarten (German), menu (French), shampoo (Hindi), bonanza (Spanish), piano (Italian), kosher (Yiddish), and smorgasbord (Swedish).

37. For an exercise in objective versus subjective writing, after a lesson on descriptive writing, bring to class a nondescript object, such as a potato, and place it before the class. Ask them to write a paragraph either describing the potato in detail, that is, its color, size, markings, and other characteristics, or describing how the potato feels about them.

38. Read a story to the class but without its ending. Then ask the students (as individuals or in think-write-share pairs) to invent and write their own endings or conclusions, and then share those.

39. Challenge students to create an advertisement (decide for radio, TV, Internet, movie theatre, or print medium) using a propaganda device of their choice.

40. Invite students (individually or in pairs) to create and design an invention and then to write a "patent description" for the invention.

41. Using think-write-share pairs, invite students individually to write a physical description of some well-known public figure, such as a movie star, politician, athlete, writer, artist, or musician. Other class members may then try to identify the "mystery" personality from the written description.

42. A bulletin board may be designated for current events and news in the world of writers. New books and recordings as well as reviews may be included. News of poets and authors (student authors and poets, too) may also be displayed.

43. Everyone has heard of or experienced stereotyping. For example: Girls are not as athletic as boys, boys are insensitive, women are better cooks than men, and men are more mechanical than women. Ask students to list stereotypes they have heard and examples they find in media. Have students discuss these questions: How do you suppose these stereotypes came to be? Does stereotyping have any useful value? Can it be harmful?

44. Remove the text from a newspaper comic strip and have the students work in pairs to create the story line, or give each pair a picture from a magazine and have the pair create a story about the picture.

45. Use newspaper and Internet want ads to locate jobs as a base for completing job application forms and creating letters of inquiry.

46. To develop language and listening skills, use video-recording equipment to record student-written employer-employee role-play situations, interviews for jobs, or child-parent situations.

47. Invite students to choose a short story from a text, write it into a play, and perform the play for their family members.

48. To begin a poetry unit, ask students to bring in the lyrics to their favorite songs. Show how these fit into the genre of poetry.

49. Invite students to analyze commercial advertisements that might be classed as "ecopornographic," that is, ads for a product that is potentially damaging to our environment.

50. Have students analyze commercial advertisements for the emotions to which they appeal, for the techniques used, and for their integrity. Try the same thing with radio, youth magazines, theater advertisements, web sites, and other media.

51. Change the learning environment by moving to an outdoor location, and ask students to write poetry to see if the change in surroundings stimulates or discourages their creativeness. Discuss the results. For example, take your class to a large supermarket to write, or to a mall, lake, forest, or athletic stadium.

52. Use your state's seal to initiate the study of the concept of interpretations. Have students analyze the seal for its history and the meaning of its various symbols.

53. Provide puppets in native costume for students to use in practicing dialogue when learning a language or in developing language skills.

54. Have students use the Internet to establish communication with students from another place in the world.

55. As a class or small-group project, design a page on your school web site.

56. Use drama to build language arts and thinking skills. Have students write dialogue, set scenes, and communicate emotions through expressive language and mime.

57. Establish a community-service learning literacy project. For example, students from Greenville High School (Greenville, TN) serve as mentors to local elementary school children to help the children develop their reading and comprehension skills, and students from Urbana High School (Urbana, IL) are trained to give one-on-one tutoring in reading to students from a local elementary school.

58. At San Altos Elementary School (Lemon Grove, CA), a kindergarten teacher uses a digital camera to take pictures of her students acting out scenes from a book being read in class. She puts the photos on slides and asks the students to describe their actions in words. From this activity the children create their own books.

59. Have students create and write a movie script by viewing any five- to ten-minute scene from a film and then writing a script for that particular scene.

60. First-graders from a school in Arizona became pen pals with inner-city second-graders from Toledo, OH. Not only did the experience prove beneficial for their lessons in language arts, but it also promoted their knowledge about their city and state, resulting in cross-curricular learning (Lemkuhl, 2002).

61. Challenge students to look for, create, and collect palindromes—a series of words, sentences, or numbers, that read the same backward or forward. Examples are the names *Ava* and *Otto,* the words *naïve and Evian,* the date *4.04.04*, and the year 2002.

Mathematics

62. Collaboratively plan with students a role-play unit where members role-play the solar system. Students calculate their weights, set up a proportion system, find a large area such as a soccer field, and as a culmination to the project actually simulate the solar system, using their own bodies to represent the sun, planets, and moons. Notify local media of the culminating event.

63. Encourage students to look for evidence of the Fibonacci number series (i.e., 1, 1, 2, 3, 5, 8, 13, 21, etc.), both within and outside mathematics, such as in nature and in manufactured objects. Here are a few examples of where evidence may be found: piano keyboard, petals of flowers, spermatogenesis and oogenesis. Perhaps your students might like to organize a Fibonacci Club and, through the Internet, establish communication with similar clubs around the world.

64. After students research the history of the cost of a first-class U.S. postage stamp, ask them to devise ways of predicting its cost by the year they graduate, the year they become grandparents, or some other target year.

65. Provide students a list of the frequencies of each of the 88 keys and strings on a piano (a local music store can provide the information). Challenge students to derive an equation to express the relation between key position and frequency. After they have done this, research and tell them about the Bösendorfer piano (Germany), with its nine extra keys at the lower end of the keyboard. See if students can predict the frequencies of those extra keys.

66. Using a light sensor to measure the intensity of a light source from various distances, have students graph the data points and then, with their scientific calculators, find the relevant equation.

67. Students can participate in a parachute creation contest. Using plastic from trash bags, string, and a bobby pin as the skydiver, the challenge is to design a parachute with the least surface area but the longest hang time.

68. Establish a service-learning project. For example, at Sunset Elementary School (Airway Heights, WA), while helping students develop skills in leadership and communication, the students are trained by adults to tutor other children in mathematics.

69. With students you already know as peer coaches, teach students how to play chess. Invite students to plan chess moves for homework, using combination theory and probability. In collaboration with an art or shop teacher, some students may wish to extend the study by creating their own chessboards and pieces.

70. Invite students to survey and map the school grounds.

Physical Education

71. Ask your students to choose individually (or in dyads) a famous athlete they most (or least) admire. A one-page report will be written about the athlete. The student will then present the attributes and/or characteristics that they admire (or dislike)

in the athlete, and how they feel they can emulate (or avoid) those qualities. After all presentations, as a class, devise two lists, one of common attributes admired, the other of qualities to avoid.

72. Have students, in cooperative learning groups, invent an exercise routine to their favorite music recording and share it with the class, discussing how they arrived at decisions along the way.

73. Divide your class into groups. Given the basic nonlocomotor skills, have each group come up with a "people machine." Each student within the group is hooked up to another demonstrating a nonlocomotor skill and adding some sort of noise to it. Have a contest for the most creative people machine.

74. Challenge students to design a balance-beam routine that has two passes on the beam and that must include: front support mount, forward roll, leap, low or high turn, visit, chassé, and cross-support dismount. These routines will be posted to show the variety of ways the different maneuvers can be put together.

75. Divide the class into groups, giving each group certain pieces of gym equipment. Challenge each group to create a new game or activity using only the equipment they are given. Let the class play their newly created games, while being mindful of student safety.

Science

76. Challenge students to create and test their own science tools and materials, such as microscopes, using stems of bamboo with a drop of water in each end, or litmus indicators using the petals of flowers.

77. Record sounds of the environment. Compare and write about day versus night sounds, fall versus spring sounds, foggy day versus sunny day sounds, busy mall versus residential back yard sounds, single residential dwelling versus multiple residential dwelling sounds. Challenge students to create essays, poetry, or music from their work.

78. With appropriate permissions and adult supervision, plan an overnight campout in which students must "live off the land" with only sleeping bags, clothing, and other essentials (water), and no electronics. (The teacher takes a cell phone for security.)

79. Plan a yearlong project where each student, or small group of students, must develop knowledge and understanding of some specific piece of technology. Each project culmination presentation must have five components: visual, oral, written, artistic, and creative.

80. Invite students to identify and use a social relationship, such as landlord-tenant relationship, to create a role-play simulation of predator-prey relationships.

81. For the first day of a life science class, give each student one live guppy in a test tube and one live cactus plant in a three-inch pot. Tell the students that the

minimum they each need to pass the course is to bring their pet plant and fish back to you during the final week of school, alive.

82. If you are a life science teacher, make sure your classroom looks like a place for studying life rather than a place of death.

83. With each student playing the role of a cell part, have students set up and perform a role-play simulation of cells.

84. Divide your class into groups, and ask each group to create an environment for an imaginary organism using discarded items from the environment. By asking questions, each group will try and learn about other groups' "mystery" organism.

85. Have each student, or student pair, "adopt" a chemical element. The student then researches that element and becomes the class expert whenever that particular substance comes up in discussion. There could be a special bulletin board for putting up questions on interesting or little-known facts about the elements.

86. Milk can be precipitated and separated, and the solid product dried to form a very hard substance that was, in the days before plastic, used to make buttons. Challenge students to make their own buttons from milk.

87. As a class or interdisciplinary team project, obtain permission to "adopt" a wetland area or some other environmental project that is located near the school.

88. Invite students to research the composition and development of familiar objects. For example, the ordinary pencil is made of cedar wood from the forests of the Pacific Northwest. The graphite is often from Montana or Mexico and is reinforced with clays from Georgia and Kentucky. The eraser is made from soybean oil, and latex from trees in South America; reinforced with pumice from California or New Mexico; and sulfur, calcium, and barium. The metal band is aluminum or brass, made from copper and zinc, and mined in several states of the United States and in several provinces of Canada. The paint to color the wood and the lacquer to make it shine are made from a variety of different minerals and metals, as is the glue that binds the wood.

89. Invite students to design posters to hang on the classroom walls to show the meaning of words used in science that are not typical of their meaning in everyday language usage—the word "theory" is an example.

90. To bridge cultural differences, challenge students to design posters to hang on the classroom walls showing potential differences in perceptions or views according to ethno science and formal science.

91. With your students, plan a community-service project. For example, elementary school children of the Powder River County School District (Broadus, MT) adopted community flower gardens and conduct an annual food drive for the needy. At Great Falls Middle School (Montague, MA), students research and produce television documentaries on subjects related to energy. The documentaries are broadcast on the local cable channel to promote energy literacy in the school and community. Students at Baldwyn Middle School

(Baldwyn, MS) plan and care for the landscaping of the local battlefield/museum, and students from Hollidaysburg Area Senior High School (Hollidaysburg, PA) cleaned up and restored a local cemetery.

92. Sometimes projects become ongoing, permanent endeavors with many spin-off projects of shorter duration. For example, what began as a science classroom project at W. H. English Middle School (Scottsburg, IN) has become what is perhaps the largest animal refuge shelter in the Midwest. As another example, located near the estuary at the mouth of the Columbia River in Wahkiakum County, Washington, students at Wahkiakum High School participate in interdisciplinary projects that have included habitat restoration, a salmon hatchery, stream restoration, tree planting, and re-creating the final leg of the historic Lewis and Clark expedition.

93. Invite students to research and produce TV documentaries on subjects related to energy, or on a health-related topic. To promote energy or health-related literacy in the school and surrounding community, a local TV channel might be willing to broadcast the documentaries.

94. During their study of atomic theory, have students read and discuss J. R. Hersey's *Hiroshima* (Random House, 1989).

95. Ask students to inquire whether a nearby zoo or SPCA, or botanical garden or commercial nursery, has an animal or plant loan program.

96. Have a group of students research from the Internet and library and report on the plant *Morinda citrifolia*.

97. Have students use bobble-head toys to explore force and motion (Foster, 2003).

Social Studies/History

98. Invite students to create and perform skits about social issues relevant to today's youth. Perform the skits at school events, at parent–teacher organization meetings, and for community groups.

99. In collaboration with your students develop a year-long three-phase project. During the first phase, students individually research the question, "Who Am I?"; during the second phase, "Who Are They?"; during the third phase, "Who Are We?"

100. Organize an Intergenerational Advocacy program in which students and senior citizens work together to make a better society for both groups (MacBain, 1996).

101. Initiate a service-learning project where, for an extended period of time, students work directly with community organizations and agencies. For example, at Columbia Elementary School (Champaign, IL), children in primary grades do art work for local hospitals, and students in grades 4 and 5 interview senior citizens and explore background experiences. At John Ford Middle School (St. Matthews, SC), students incorporate The Constitutional

Right Foundation "City Youth" program into the curriculum, helping to make decisions about areas of the community that need improvement.

102. During the study of ancient Egypt, invite students to create and build their own model pyramids; in science, students could study simple machines that will help in their pyramid building.

103. Invite students to plan how they would improve their living environment, beginning with the classroom; moving out to the school, home, community, state, country; and ending with the global.

104. Start a pictorial essay on the development of and/or changes in a given area in your community, such as a major corner or block adjacent to the school. This is a study project that could continue for years and that has many social, political, and economic implications.

105. Invite students in small groups or as a class project to build a model that represents their community.

106. Start a folk hero study. Each year ask, "What prominent human being who has lived during (a particular period of time) do you most (and/or least) admire?" Collect individual responses to the question, tally results, and discuss. After you have done this for several years, you may wish to share with your class for discussion purposes the results of surveys of previous years.

107. Start a sister class relationship with another similar class from another school around the country or the world.

108. During the study of westward expansion, challenge students to organize a role-play of a simulated family movement to the West in the 1800s. What items would they take? What would they toss out of the wagon to lighten the load? Where would they stop and settle? Or would they stop, turn around, and return to their point of origin? What issues would enter into their decision-making?

109. Invite students to collect music, art, or athletic records from a particular period of history. Have them compare their collections with the music, art, or records of today and predict the music, art, or records of the future.

110. Using play money, establish a capitalistic economic system within your classroom. Salaries may be paid for attendance and bonus income for work well done, taxes may be collected for poor work, and a welfare section established.

111. Divide your class into small groups, asking that each group make predictions about what world governments, world geography, world social issues, world health, world energy, or some other related topic will be like some time in the future. Let each group give its report, followed by debate and discussion. With guidance from the school administration, plant the predictions in some secret location on the school grounds for a future reading.

112. As an opener to a unit on the U.S. Constitution, have students design their own classroom "bill of rights."

113. On one day, behave toward your students in class as if your class were a socialist society; the next day, as if they were a fascist society; on another day, as a communist society; etc. At the end of the simulation, have students discuss and compare their feelings and thoughts about each day's experience.

114. Using Legos™ or sugar cubes as construction blocks, and with assigned roles, challenge students to simulate the building of the Great Wall of China.

115. At Indian Trail Junior High School (Addison, IL), all eighth-graders and teachers from not only social studies but also English, mathematics, physical education, and science work together on a "real world," problem-based project titled the Inspector Red Ribbon Unit. The unit focuses on a real social problem—the prom night automobile accident.

116. Establish a caring antiviolence program. For example, high school students in Lynn Haven, FL, work as tutors/mentors with elementary school children to help boost confidence and self-esteem between both groups of students.

117. During an interdisciplinary thematic unit of study (the history and literature of the medieval period of Europe), have students study and build model castles.

118. With guidance from teachers and using a common philosophical approach based on Glasser's choice theory, reality therapy, and ideas from his other writings, students of eighth-grade history at Longfellow Middle School (La Crosse, WI) designed and built their own middle school nation (Frost, Olson, & Valiquette, 2000).

119. At Davis Senior High School (Davis, CA), students in U.S. history are given this assignment for an activity titled "Creating a Candidate." "Research electronic and print media about the progressive movement in early California history. Determine relevant issues a candidate for governor of the state in 1910 would need to address. Create a fictitious candidate. Your exhibition must include: (a) an election poster, (b) a slogan, (c) a theme song that you must sing, and (d) a five-minute platform speech addressing the issues, your proposed solutions, and the position of your opponents."

120. During the study of the U.S. Constitution, invite students to organize debates on current issues, such as gun control and civil rights.

121. Initiate a service learning project, where for an extended period of time students work directly with one or more community organizations.

122. In collaboration with other classes, invite your students to design and implement a schoolwide conflict resolution program.

123. Plan time each day if teaching elementary, or once a week if teaching secondary, for students to comment on the day's (or week's) activities, or to compliment a peer.

124. Challenge students to design and conduct a study to determine how well students who have arrived in the United States from other countries are integrated into your community and/or school's culture.

125. Challenge students to identify and discuss current plagiarism and copyright issues.

Figure 6: Internet sites for teaching ideas

Miscellaneous
- Gender bias http://www.american.edu/sadker
- *Global Schoolhouse* http://www.gsh.org
- *globalEDGE™* http://globaledge.msu.edu
- *Intercultural E-Mail Classroom Connections* http://www.iecc.org/
- Learning theories http://tip.psychology.org/theories.html
- *PBS Teacher Source* http://www.pbs.org/teachersource
- Teachers Helping Teachers http://www.pacific.net/~mandel/index.html
- *Teachers Net Lesson Bank* http://teachers.net/lessons
- *The Library in the Sky* http://www.nwrel.org/sky

Arts
- *American Alliance for Theatre & Education* http://www.aate.com/
- *Association of Theatre Movement Educators* http://www.asu.edu/cfa/atme/
- *Crayola Creativity Center* http://www.crayola.com
- Dance links http://www.SapphireSwan.com/dance/
- *Music Education Resource Links*
    http://www.isd77.k12.mn.us/resources/staffpages/shirk/k12.music.html
- *World Wide Arts Resources* http://wwar.com/

Environmental Issues
- North American Association for Environmental Education
    http://www.naaee.org
- World Bank's site http://www.worldbank.org/depweb

History/Social Studies
- Albert Shanker Institute http://www.shankerinstitute.org
- *American Women's History*
    http://frank.mtsu.edu/~kmiddlet/history/women.html
- Best of History Web Sites http://www.besthistorysites.net
- Choices Program http://www.choices.edu/index.cfm
- Civics Online http://civics-online.org
- Facing History and Ourselves http://facinghistory.org
- *FedWorld* http://www.fedworld.gov
- *Historical Text Archive* http://historicaltextarchive.com
- *History Net* http://www.thehistorynet.com
- *Houghton Mifflin Social Studies Center* http://www.eduplace.com/ss/
- Links to lesson plans, unit plans, thematic units, and resources
    http://www.csun.edu/~hcedu013/index.html
- *Mexico Online* http://www.mexonline.com
- National Council for the Social Studies http://www.socialstudies.org
- *Scrolls from the Dead Sea*
    http://sunsite.unc.edu/expo/deadsea.scrolls.exhibit/intro.html
- *Social Science Resources* http://www.nde.state.ne.us/SS/ss.html

---

- U.S. History, *From Revolution to Reconstruction*
  http://grid.let.rug.nl/~welling/usa/usa.html

Language and Literacy http://www.uis.edu/~cook/langlit/index.html
- Language links http://polyglot.lss.wisc.edu/lss/lang/langlink.html
- Literacy Matters project http://www.literacymatters.org
- National Clearinghouse for English Language Acquisition & Language
  Instruction Education Programs http://www.ncela.gwu.edu
- National Writing Project http://www.writingproject.org
- ReadWriteThink http://www.readwritethink.org
- Second language learning http://www.sdkrashen.com
- WritingFix http://www.writingfix.com

Mathematics
- Fun Mathematics Lessons http://www.math.rice.edu/~lanius/Lessons
- Math Activities http://www.k111.k12.il.us/king/math.htm
- *Math Archives* http://archives.math.utk.edu
- Math for Elementary Teachers
  http://www.mtlakes.org/ww/tech/webtools/math.htm
- *Math Forum* http://forum.swarthmore.edu/
- Mathematics Lesson Plans K-12 http://www.coled.org/cur/math.html#math3
- *MathSource (Wolfram)* http://mathsource.wri.com
- Mega Mathematics http://www.c3.lanl.gov/mega-math
- *PlaneMath* http://www.planemath.com
- Show-Me Project http://www.showmecenter.missouri.edu

Science and Health
- Centers for Disease Control and Prevention; National Center on Birth Defects
  and Developmental Disabilities http://www.cdc.gov/ncbddd
- *Columbia Education Center* K-12 lesson plan collection http://www.col-
  ed.org/cur/science.html#sci1
- *Dive and Discover* http://www.divediscover.whoi.edu
- *Electronic Zoo* http://netvet.wustl.edu/e-zoo.htm
- EXCITE (Excellence in Curriculum Integration through Teaching
  Epidemiology http://www.cdc.gov/excite
- LifeQuest Expedition http://www.thequestnetwork.com
- Mandel's collection http://www.pacificnet.net/~mandel/Science.html
- National Institutes of Health http://science.education.nih.gov
- National Institute on Alcohol Abuse and Alcoholism http://www.niaaa.nih.gov
- Stanford Solar Center http://solar-center.stanford.edu
- Windows to the Universe http://www.windows.umich.edu

Publishers of Student Writing
- *New Moon* (for girls ages 8-14) http://www.newmoon.org
- *Potato Hill Poetry* (all grades) http://www.potatohill.com/contest.html
- *Stone Soup* http://www.stonesoup.com/index.html

- *What If* (for Canadians) http://www.whatifmagazine.com
- *Word Dance* (for grades K-8) http://www.worddance.com

Service Learning
- Learning In Deed http://www.learningindeed.org
- National Service-Learning Clearinghouse http://www.servicelearning.org
- National Service-Learning Exchange http://www.nslexchange

PAPERWORK: HOW TO AVOID BECOMING BURIED UNDER MOUNDS OF IT

A downfall for some beginning teachers is that of being buried under mounds of student papers to be read and graded, leaving less and less time for effective planning. To keep this from happening to you, consider the following suggestions.

Although I believe in providing second opportunity options and that the teacher should read almost everything that students write, papers can be read with varying degrees of intensity and scrutiny, depending on the purpose of the assignment. For assignments that are designed for learning, understanding, and practice, you can allow students to check them themselves using either self-checking or peer-checking. During the self- or peer-checking, you can walk around the room, monitor the activity, and record whether a student did the assignment or not, or, after the checking, you can collect the papers and do a quick read and your recording. Besides reducing the amount of paperwork for you, student self- or peer-checking provides other advantages: (1) it allows students to see and understand their errors, (2) it encourages productive peer dialogue, and (3) it helps them develop self-assessment techniques and standards. If, however, the purpose of the assignment is to assess mastery competence, then the papers should be read, marked, and graded only by you.

TEACHING VIGNETTE
No One Truly Knowledgeable About It Ever Said That Good Teaching Is Easy

Sarah is a sixth-grade teacher in a low SES school in a moderately large city of Texas. Her 34 students include ten limited-English speakers and eight with identified learning problems. Some of the students have reading and comprehension skills as low as primary grades. In any given week, Sarah recycles newspapers and sells snacks to pay for field trips because the school and the children can't. On a typical school day recently, Sarah began her work at school at 7:00 a.m. with three parent conferences. The students arrived and school started at 8:15 and ran until 2:45 p.m. Sarah then tutored several students until 3:45, conducted three more parent conferences, and entered data into her classroom desk computer before going home at 6 p.m. In the evening she planned lessons and graded papers for another two hours before retiring for the night.

Cautions About Using Peer-Checking

Peer-checking can, however, be a problem. During peer-checking of student work, students may spend more time watching the person checking their paper than accurately checking the one given to them. And this strategy does not necessarily allow the student to see or understand his or her mistakes.

The issue of privacy is perhaps an even greater concern. When Student A becomes knowledgeable of the academic success or failure of Student B, Student A, the "checker," could cause emotional or social embarrassment to Student B. Peer-checking of papers should perhaps be done only for editing of classmates' drafts of stories or research projects, making suggestions about content and grammar, but not assigning a grade or marking answers right or wrong. To protect students' privacy rights, the use of peers grading each other's papers also should be avoided. Harassment and embarrassment do not support a positive and safe learning environment.

PARENT AND GUARDIAN CONTACTS AND INVOLVEMENT: LEAVE NO PARENT/GUARDIAN BEHIND

When parents (or guardians) are involved in their child's school and school work, students learn better and earn better grades, and teachers experience more positive feelings about teaching. Knowing this, schools increasingly are searching for new and better ways to involve parents, guardians, and even grandparents.

Some teachers make a point to contact parents or guardians by telephone or by electronic mail, especially when a student has shown a sudden turn for either the worse or the better in academic achievement or in classroom behavior. That initiative by the teacher is usually welcomed by the adults and can lead to productive conferences with the teacher. A telephone conference can save valuable time for both you and the parent or guardian.

I firmly believe in the value of relaying positive news to parents or guardians, and doing so just as often as for conveying information that is not positive. Relaying positive news is for your own mental health as much as it is for the good of the children and their parents or guardians.

Another way of contacting parents/guardians is by letter. Making contact by letter gives you time to think and to make clear your thoughts and concerns to that parent and to invite the parent to respond at her or his convenience by letter, phone, or arranging to have a conference with you. Regarding the latter, you can give out the school phone number and your school e-mail address, but be advised to *never* give your home address or personal phone number.

Value Differences: Avoid Being Judgmental

How you view people from cultures different from you will have a profound effect on how you work with those children and the adult members of their family. To work most successfully with all children and their parents/guardians, it is exceedingly important that you clearly and openly value cultural differences, demonstrating respect and your vision of equality for those adults regardless of how they might differ from you. Keep in mind your shared ultimate goal—to help their children learn and succeed in life.

Back-to-School Night and Open House

You will meet some parents or guardians early in the school year during Back-to-School or Meet-the-Teacher or Curriculum Night and throughout the year in individual parent conferences and during spring open house. For the beginning teacher, these can be anxious times. But in fact, it is a time to celebrate your work and to solicit help from parents.

Back-to-School Night is the evening early in the school year when parents and guardians come to the school and meet their children's teachers. The adults arrive at the student's home base and then proceed through a simulation of their sons' or daughters' school day; as a group, they meet each class and each teacher for a few minutes. Later, in the spring, there is an open house where parents and other adults may have more time to talk individually with teachers, although the major purpose of the open house is for the school and teachers to celebrate the work and progress of the students for that year. Throughout the school year, there will be opportunities for you and parents/guardians to meet and to talk about their child. Never hesitate to solicit the help of a language interpreter whenever you anticipate there might be a need.

At Back-to-School Night, parents are eager to learn as much as they can about their children's teachers. You will meet each group of adults for a brief time, perhaps about ten minutes. During that meeting, you will provide them with a copy of the course syllabus (if you are an upper grade teacher); make some straightforward remarks about yourself; and talk about the class or course, its requirements, your expectations of the students, and how the parents or guardians might help.

Although there will be precious little time for questions from the parents, during your introduction, the parents will be delighted to learn that you have your program well planned, are a "task master," appreciate their interest and welcome their inquiries and participation, and will communicate with them.

Specifically, parents and guardians will expect to learn about your curriculum—goals and objectives, any long-term projects, when tests will be given and if given on a regular basis, and your grading procedures. They will want to know what you expect of them: Is there homework, and if so, should they help their children with it? How can they contact you? Try to anticipate other questions. Your principal, department chair, or colleagues can help you anticipate and prepare for these questions. Of course, you can never prepare for the question that comes from left field. Just remain calm and avoid being flustered (or at least appear to be calm). Ten minutes will fly by quickly, and parents/guardians will be reassured to know you are an in-control teacher.

Finally, just as when you are working with the children in your class, if a parent or guardian asks a question for which you do not have an answer, *never* bluff an answer. When asked a question for which you do not have an answer, one response is,

"I don't know; does anyone care to respond?" With parents and guardians, you can promise them that you will find the answer and then let them know.

Conferences

When meeting parents and guardians for conferences, you should be as specific as possible when explaining to them the progress of their child in your class. And, again, express your appreciation for their interest. Be helpful to their understanding, and don't saturate them with more information than they need. Resist any tendency to talk too much. Allow time for the parent or guardian to ask questions. Keep your answers succinct. Never compare one student with another or with the rest of the class. If the parent asks a question for which you do not have an answer, tell the parent you will try to find an answer and will phone the parent as quickly as you can. And do it. Have the student's portfolio and other work with you during the adult conference so you can show the parent or guardian examples of what is being discussed. Also, have your grade book on hand, or a computer printout of it, but be prepared to protect from the parent the names and records of the other students.

Sometimes it is helpful to have a three-way conference: a conference with the parent or guardian, the student, and you, or a conference with the parent/guardian, the principal or counselor, and several or all of the student's teachers. If, especially as a beginning teacher, you would like the presence of an administrator at a parent-teacher conference, don't hesitate to arrange that.

Some educators prefer a student-led conference. But, like most innovations in education, the concept of student-led conferences has its limitations—the most important of which perhaps is the matter of time.

Dealing with an Angry Parent or Guardian

Dealing with an angry or hostile parent or guardian can be scary for any teacher, but especially for a novice teacher. Never hesitate to ask the school principal to be present during the conference if that will make you feel more comfortable. The paragraphs that follow offer guidelines for dealing with a hostile parent or guardian.

Remain calm in your discussion with the parent, allowing the parent to talk out his or her hostility while you say very little; usually, the less you say, the better off you will be. What you do say must be objective and to the point of the child's work in your classroom. The parent may just need to vent frustrations that might have very little to do with you, the school, or even the child.

Avoid allowing yourself to be intimidated, put on the defensive, or backed into a verbal corner. If the parent tries to do so by attacking you personally, do not press your defense at this point. Perhaps the parent has made a point that would be worthwhile for you to take time to consider; this may be a good time to arrange for another conference with the parent for about a week later. In a follow-up conference, if the parent agrees, you may want to consider bringing in a mediator, such as another member of your teaching team, an administrator, or a school counselor or psychologist.

Avoid talking about other students; keep the conversation focused on this parent's child's progress. The parent is *not* or should not be your rival. You both share a concern for the academic and emotional well-being of the child. Use your best skills in critical thinking and problem solving, trying to focus the discussion by identifying the problem, defining it, and then arriving at a decision about how mutually to go about solving it. To this end, you may need to ask for help from a third party, such as the child's school counselor. If agreed to by the parent or guardian, please take that step.

POLITICS AT SCHOOL: BEST TO AVOID

Sometimes, because of philosophical differences, power struggles, and political tensions within a school staff, a beginning teacher's struggles can become clouded with issues other than the usual ones concerning curriculum and student behavior. My advice: Develop as quickly as possible a support network made up of both colleagues at school and friends outside the school who can support you in your work. Try to avoid political issues and power struggles. As a beginning teacher, you can't afford the time, alienation, or emotional drain that involvement might cause.

PROFESSIONAL ORGANIZATIONS: JOIN ONE

There are many professional organizations, general and discipline-specific—local, statewide, and national—and their programs, publications, and services can be valuable to a beginning teacher. Most have a web page on the Internet. I suggest that because, as a first-year teacher, it is most likely that you are far from being wealthy, you investigate carefully all the possibilities, then select and join the one professional organization that you believe will be most helpful and supportive for your work as a beginning teacher. You may be entitled to a reduced membership rate if you are an enrolled university student.

PROTECTING STUDENTS AND YOURSELF: LIABILITY, SAFETY, AND SECURITY MATTERS

You need to be aware of potential liability and safety issues that can arise, especially from chauffeuring students, admitting them into your home, or simply being alone with a student. To prevent problems, *avoid doing any of those things*.

To best protect your students, and yourself, you must be knowledgeable about legal guidelines for public school teaching and about teacher and student rights, be steadily alert for potential safety hazards, and be knowledgeable about what you should or should not do in an emergency situation. Beyond the brief presentation that follows, you will want to continue to increase your awareness about these and similar matters by talking with experienced teachers, reading, and attending workshops or classes where these and similar topics are addressed in detail.

Student Rights

Students should be informed of their rights by their schools (many schools provide students with a publication of their rights), and they should be encouraged to report any suspected violations of their rights to the school principal or other designated person.

You are likely aware that federal law prohibits any discrimination against individuals with disabilities or discrimination that is based on race, color, national origin, or gender. In all aspects of school, students must be treated the same. This means, for example, that a teacher must not pit males against females in a subject-content quiz game—or for any other activity or reason. Further, no teacher, student, administrator, or other school employee should make sexual advances toward or sexually harass a student (e.g., speaking or touching in a sexual manner). The school and classroom atmosphere must be one of trust, dignity, and respect among students and the adult staff.

Teacher Liability and Insurance

You are probably protected by your school district against personal injury litigation (i.e., a negligence suit filed as the result of a student being injured at school or at a school-sponsored activity). However, you may want to investigate the extent of your tort (i.e., any private or civil wrong for which a civil suit can be brought) liability coverage. You may decide that the coverage provided by the district is insufficient. Additional liability coverage can be obtained through private insurance agents and through many of the larger national teacher's organizations.

Teachers sometimes find themselves in situations where they are tempted to transport students in their own private automobiles, such as for field trips and other off-campus activities. Before ever transporting students in your automobile—or in private automobiles driven by volunteer adults—you and other drivers should inquire from your insurance agents whether you have adequate automobile insurance liability coverage to do that and if any written permissions or release from liability is needed. My advice is simply to avoid using your own vehicle to transport students.

Inevitably, teachers take personal items to school—purses, cameras, CD players, and so forth. It is unlikely that the school's insurance policy covers your personal items if they are stolen or damaged. A homeowner's or apartment renter's policy might. My advice is to avoid taking valuable personal items to school. Those items you must have with you, such as keys, should be well protected from being misplaced, lost, or stolen.

Child Abuse

Child abuse is a grave matter of urgent national concern. Although physical abuse is the easiest to detect, other abuse (e.g., incest, improper nutrition, improper clothing, unattended medical problems, and inadequate dental care) can be just as serious. *In all states, teachers are legally mandated to report any suspicion of child abuse.*

Report your suspicion by telephoning toll free 1-800-4-A-CHILD (1-800-422-4453), the National Child Abuse Hotline. Proof of abuse is unnecessary.

Any student who comes to your classroom abused needs to feel welcome and secure while in the classroom. For additional information, contact experts from your local school district, the state department of education, or a nearby Children's Protective Services (CPS) agency.

First Aid and Medication

Accidents and resulting injuries to students at school do occur. While doing a science laboratory experiment, a student is burned by a nearly colorless flame. In an English class, a student is cut by glass from a falling windowpane when the teacher attempts to open a stuck window. While playing on the playground during recess, a child falls and lands face down on a lawn sprinkler head that had remained upright, although the water was off. On the athletic field, a student is hit by a falling goal post weakened as the result of termite action below the surface. A student breaks an arm when she falls after another student pulls her chair out from beneath her. Do you understand what you should do when a student under your supervision is injured?

First, you should give first aid *only* when necessary to save a limb or life. When life or limb is not at risk, then you should follow school policy by referring the student immediately to professional care. When immediate professional care is unavailable and you believe that immediate first aid is necessary, then you can take prudent action, as if you were that student's parent or legal guardian. But you must always be cautious and knowledgeable about what you are doing so that you do not cause further injury.

Unless you are a licensed medical professional, you should *never* give medication to a minor, whether prescription or over-the-counter. Students who need to take personal medication should bring from home a written parental statement of permission and instructions. Under your supervision as the student's classroom teacher—or that of the school nurse (if there is one)—the student can then take the medicine.

RECORDS: ORGANIZATION IS IMPORTANT TO SUCCESS

If you are not an organized person, then as quickly as possible do what is necessary to become one. If necessary, find a colleague who seems to be well organized and ask how that person does it.

Record Keeping

You must maintain well-organized and complete records of student achievement. You may do this in a written record book or on an electronic record book. At the very least, the record book should include attendance and tardy records and all records of student scores on tests, homework, projects, and other assignments. In addition, I advise you to maintain a log and written record with copies of everything you communicate to parents and to school personnel (e.g., administrator, counselor, or school nurse).

Worst Nightmare

One reason for maintaining records is to be prepared to defend yourself if accused of misbehavior by a student, perhaps in retribution for something you did. Here are two recent examples, each involving a new teacher and eighth-grade students.

A male beginning teacher was accused first by one eighth-grade female student, then by five other female students who joined her, of unwanted staring at the girls—in effect, of sexual harassment. The student who initiated the accusation had been caught by the teacher twice during the previous week cheating in class on a test and on an assignment. In speaking of the teacher, she also had written in her journal, "Let's get this bozo." Although the teacher's documentation and a conference with the school principal and the girl's parents helped to resolve the matter quickly in the teacher's favor, it still was an anxious and very unsettling experience for the new teacher, who, upon reflection, is uncertain whether he wants to continue in the profession.

In another situation, after a teacher had accused an eighth-grade student of forging notes from home, in retribution the student wrote on an assignment, "Let's get him out of here." The student's parents phoned the school principal complaining that the teacher had unfairly accused their son of dishonesty. In a conference with the teacher, principal, and student's parents, the issue was resolved when the teacher apologized for his accusation. However, the teacher had lost rapport with this particular class. The bottom line: Never accuse a student of cheating unless you have absolute proof.

RELIABILITY: A GOOD TEACHER IS A DEPENDABLE PERSON

Make no commitments you cannot fulfill. You want to be considered as a person who is reliable, who consistently fulfills professional responsibilities, promises, and commitments. A teacher who cannot be relied on is quick to lose credibility with the students (as well as with colleagues, administrators, and parents). An unreliable teacher is an incompetent teacher. And, for whatever reason, a teacher who is chronically absent from his or her teaching duties is an at-risk teacher—that is, one who is on the verge of dropping out of the profession.

SALARY: NOT GREAT BUT REGULAR

Sometimes beginning teachers become disenchanted with their career choice because of the beginning salary, which for some is impossible to live on, especially for the teacher with a family to support. Unfortunately, a beginning teacher with a family to support may have to moonlight to support the teaching income, and that takes time and energy from the teacher's devotion to teaching.

Salaries for beginning teachers are not great. However, as a teacher, your income will likely be steady, coming in every month, and will increase steadily throughout your career, which may be for 30 or more years. Teachers are seldom laid off or fired; even, unfortunately, those who are grossly incompetent. In addition, many teachers are able to supplement their regular teaching income with additional income from summer or intersession teaching or other school-related tasks.

SENSE OF HUMOR, AN INTELLIGENT BEHAVIOR: PLEASE SMILE AND DO SO LONG BEFORE CHRISTMAS

Students appreciate and learn more from a teacher who shares a sense of humor and smiles and laughs with the students. The positive effects of appropriate humor (i.e., humor that is not self-deprecating or disrespectful of others) on learning and living are well established: drop in the pulse rate; reduction of feelings of anxiety, tension, and stress; secretion of endorphins; and an increase in blood oxygen. Humor and laughter increases immune system activity and decreases stress-producing hormones. It causes an increase in the activity of the body's natural cells that attack and kill tumor cells and viruses. It activates T-cells for the immune system, antibodies that fight against harmful microorganisms, and gamma interferon, a hormone that fights viruses and regulates cell growth. Because of these effects, humor relaxes us, helps us to stay healthy, and encourages creativity and higher-level thinking. Humor is an intelligent behavior that should be cherished and nourished.

CLASSROOM VIGNETTE
A Humorous Scenario: A Missed Teachable Moment

While Emily was reciting, she had some difficulty with her throat (due to a cold) and stumbled over some words. The teacher jokingly commented, "That's okay Emily, you must have a frog in your throat." Quickly, Mariya, a recent newcomer from the Ukraine, queried, "How could Emily have a frog in her throat?" The teacher ignored Mariya's question. Missing this teachable moment, the teacher continued with the planned lesson.

STUDENT ACHIEVEMENT: THE IMPORTANT AND TIME-INTENSIVE RESPONSIBILITIES OF ASSESSING, GRADING, AND REPORTING

The development of the student encompasses growth in three domains—the cognitive, affective, and psychomotor. Traditional objective paper-and-pencil tests provide only a portion of the data needed to indicate student progress in learning.

Various techniques of assessment should be used to determine how the student works, what the student is learning, and what the student can produce as a result of that learning.

While assessment of cognitive domain learning lends itself to traditional written tests of achievement, the assessment of learning within the affective and psychomotor domains is best suited by the use of performance rubric (standards) checklists, student behaviors can be observed in action. However, many teachers today are using alternative assessment procedures (i.e., alternatives to traditional paper-and-pencil written testing). After all, for learning that is most important and that has the most meaning to students, the domains are inextricably interconnected. Learning that is meaningful to students is not as easily compartmentalized, as taxonomies of educational objectives would imply. Alternative assessment strategies include the use of projects, portfolios, skits, papers, oral presentations, and performance tests. Performance rubric checklists can be prepared for use with any of those strategies.

Avenues for Assessing Student Learning

For assessing a student's achievement in learning, the three general avenues are (1) assess what the student *says*—e.g., the quantity and quality of a student's contributions to class discussions; (2) assess what the student *does*—e.g., the amount and quality of a student's participation in the learning activities; and (3) assess what the student *writes (or draws)*—e.g., as shown by items in the student's portfolio (e.g., homework assignments, checklists, project work, and written tests). Although your own situation and personal philosophy will dictate the levels of importance and weight you give to each avenue of assessment, you should have a strong rationale if you value and weigh the three avenues for assessment differently than one-third each.

With each assessment strategy used, you are advised to proceed from your awareness of anticipated learning outcomes (the learning objectives) and to assess a student's progress toward meeting those objectives. That is assessment that is *criterion-referenced*.

Assessing What a Student Says and Does. When assessing what a student says, you should (a) *listen* to the student's oral reports, questions, responses, and interactions with others and (b) *observe* the student's attentiveness, involvement in class activities, creativeness, and responses to challenges. Notice that I say you should listen and observe. While listening to what the student is saying, you should be observing the student's nonverbal behaviors. When assessing a student's verbal and nonverbal behaviors in the classroom, you should:

- Maintain an anecdotal record (teacher's log) book or folder, with a separate section in it for your records of each student.

- For a specific activity, list the desirable behaviors.

- Check the list against the specific instructional objectives.

- Record your observations as quickly as possible following your observation. Audio or video recordings and, of course, software programs are available that can help

77

you maintain records and check the accuracy of your memory, but if this is inconvenient, you should spend time during school, immediately after school, or later that evening recording your observations while they are still fresh in your memory.

- Record your professional judgment about the student's progress toward the desired behavior.

- Write comments that are reminders to yourself, such as "Discuss observation with the student," "Discuss observations with student's mentor" (e.g., an adult from the community), and "Discuss observations with colleagues."

Assessing What a Student Writes (or Draws). When assessing what a student writes, you can use worksheets, written homework and papers, journal writing, writing projects, portfolios, and tests.

Student assignments and test items should correlate with and be compatible with specific instructional objectives (i.e., they should be criterion-referenced). Any given objective may be checked by using more than one method and by using more than one instrument. Subjectivity, inherent in the assessment process, may be reduced as you check for validity, comparing results of one measuring strategy against those of another.

Provide written or verbal comments about the student's work, and be positive in those comments. Rather than just writing "good" on a student's paper, briefly state what it was about it that made it good. Rather than simply saying or pointing out that the student didn't do it correctly, tell or show the student what is acceptable and how to achieve it.

Think First, Write Second: That Which Separates the Professional Teacher from Anyone Off the Street Is the Teacher's Ability to Go Beyond Mere Description of Behavior

Think carefully about written comments that you intend to make about a student. Young people can be quite sensitive to what others say about them, and most particularly to comments about them made by a teacher. It very well may be that for some students you may be the only adult in their lives that they hold in high regard. Cherish and protect that potentiality.

Think before writing a comment on a student's paper, asking yourself how you believe the student (or a parent or guardian) will interpret and react to the comment and if that is a correct interpretation or reaction to your intended meaning.

Comments carelessly, hurriedly, and thoughtlessly made by you can be detrimental to a student's welfare and progress in school. Your comments must be professional; that is, they must be diagnostically useful to the continued intellectual and psychological development of the student. This is true for any comment you make or write, whether on a student's paper, or on the student's permanent school record, or on a message sent to the student's home. That which separates the professional teacher from anyone off the street is the teacher's ability to go beyond mere description of behavior. Keep that thought in mind always when you write comments that will be read by students, by their parents or guardians, and by other educators.

Student Journals and Assessment

When reading student journals, avoid correcting grammar and spelling, and avoid writing evaluative comments or grades in the journals. Comments and evaluations from teachers might discourage creative and spontaneous expression. You may talk individually with students to seek clarification about their expressions. Student journals are useful in understanding the student's thought processes and writing skills (diagnostic assessment) and should not be graded. For grading purposes, you may simply record whether the student is maintaining a journal and, perhaps, a judgment about the quantity of writing in it, but no judgment should be made by you about its quality. Student journals are for encouraging students to write (or draw), to think about their thinking (metacognition), and to record their creative thoughts. Encourage students to write about their experiences, especially about their experiences as related to what is being learned. Writing in journals gives them practice in expressing themselves in written form and in connecting their learning and should provide nonthreatening freedom to do it.

Student Portfolios and Assessment

When reviewing student portfolios, discuss with students individually the progress in their learning as shown by the materials in their portfolios. As with student journals, the portfolio should not be graded or compared in any way with those of other students. Its purpose is for student self-assessment and to show progress in learning. For this to happen, students should keep in their portfolios all or major samples of work that is related to the class.

Avoiding the Rush at the End of a Grading Period

If you teach in an upper grade, you may be able to plan to end your own grading period a week before the quarter or semester ends and thus prevent the rush of having to read, score, and record papers; to convert scores to quarter grades for reporting; and to complete the reporting forms that must be turned in to the office.

Report Cards

Early in the school year, preferably before the students arrive that first day but long before the end of the first reporting period, you need to learn about your district or school requirements regarding procedures for reporting student achievement. Not learning of the requirements and procedures related to reporting until the end of a reporting period can be a nightmare for the teacher who has not planned for them and gathered needed forms and information.

STUDENT LEARNING: WHEN STUDENTS DO NOT LEARN THE WAY WE TEACH THEM, THEN WE MUST TEACH THEM THE WAY THEY LEARN

So advises researcher and author Rita Dunn (1995, p. 30). Learning modality refers to the sensory portal means (or input channel) by which a student prefers to receive sensory reception (modality preference) or the actual way a student learns best (modality adeptness). Some students prefer learning by seeing, a *visual modality*; others prefer learning through instruction from others (through talk), an *auditory modality*; while many others prefer learning by doing and being physically involved, referred to as *kinesthetic modality*, and by touching objects, the *tactile modality*. Sometimes a student's modality preference is not that student's modality strength.

While primary modality strength can be determined from observing students, it can also be mixed, and it also can change as the result of experience and intellectual maturity. As one might suspect, *modality integration* (i.e., engaging more of the sensory input channels, using several modalities at once or staggered) has been found to contribute to better achievement in student learning.

Because many young people neither have a preference nor strength for auditory reception, teachers should severely limit their use of telling, especially the use of the lecture method of instruction. Furthermore, instruction that uses a singular approach, such as auditory (e.g., lecturing to the students), cheats students who learn better another way. This difference can affect student achievement. A teacher, for example, who relies solely on talk, lectures and discussions, day after day, is shortchanging the education of students who learn better another way, who are, for example, kinesthetic and visual learners.

As a general rule, young people prefer and learn best by touching objects, by feeling shapes and textures, moving things around, and by interacting with each other. In contrast, learning by sitting and listening are difficult for many of them. As an example, read the following vignette about how students in one chemistry class learned about the discovery of oxygen, thinking about how it compares with the more traditional approach where the teacher stood before the class lecturing to them about the discovery.

CLASSROOM VIGNETTE
Students Write and Stage a One-Act Play

Early in the school year, in preparation for a unit on the study of oxygen, Mario told the 28 students in his high school chemistry class that if they were interested, he would like for them to plan, write, and stage a one-act play about the life of Joseph Priestley. Priestley was a theologian and scientist who in 1774 discovered what he called "dephlogisticated air," later named oxygen by Lavoisier. Furthermore, the students would be given two weeks to plan. The play would be presented and videotaped in class. Accepting Mario's idea with enthusiasm, the students immediately went about the task of organizing and putting their ideas into motion. They accepted the challenging task with such vigor and seriousness that they asked

Mario for an additional three days to make final preparations. Matthew, a bright student who was really more interested in drama than in science, was selected by his peers to play the role of Priestley and to also be the producer. Other students played lesser roles. Students with special interest in writing wrote the script. Those with interest in art and stagecraft assumed the tasks of designing and preparing the set, while another became the sound stage manager. The resulting 60-minute presentation was more successful than Mario, and perhaps the students, had anticipated—so much so that by request of the school principal, the students performed the play twice again, once for the entire student body, a second time for the parents, guardians, and community. Both performances resulted in standing ovations. During the community performance the production was simultaneously recorded by the local cable television network and later played several times over the community cable channel. Mario later said that during this experience, the students learned far more content than they ever would have via his traditional approach to the topic, plus these students were highly motivated in chemistry class for the rest of the school year. Matthew, several years later, graduated with honors from the University of California at Berkeley with a degree major in theatre and a minor in chemistry.

Students at Risk: Integration of Learning Modalities Is a Must

The term *at risk* is used to identify students who have a high probability of not completing their formal K-12 education. Researchers have identified five categories of factors that cause a young person to be at risk. These categories are personal pain (exemplified by drugs, abuse, suspension from school), academic failure, family tragedy, family socioeconomic situation (exemplified by low income, negativism, lack of education), and family instability (exemplified by frequent moves, separation, and divorce) (Tiedt & Tiedt, 1995). Many students, at any one time, have risk factors from more than one of these categories. It has been estimated that 2020, the majority of students in the public schools in this country will be at risk (Rossi & Stringfield, 1995). Today's movement to transform schools into caring, responsive, and productive learning environments has, as its sole purpose, that of helping every child succeed in school and in life.

As you prepare your own classroom and instructional plans, keep in mind that students who are underachieving and at risk need (a) frequent opportunities for mobility; (b) options and choices; (c) a variety of instructional resources, environments, and sociological groupings, rather than routines and patterns; (d) to learn during late morning, afternoon, or evening hours, rather than in the early morning; (e) informal seating, rather than wooden, steel, or plastic chairs; (f) low illumination, because bright light contributes to hyperactivity; and (g) tactile/visual introductory resources reinforced by kinesthetic (i.e., direct experiencing and whole-body activities)/visual resources, or introductory kinesthetic/visual resources reinforced by tactile/visual resources (Dunn, 1995).

You are advised to use strategies that integrate the modalities. When they are well designed, thematic units and project-based learning—as done, for example, in "Students Write and Stage a One-Act Play"--incorporate modality integration. In conclusion, then, when teaching a group of students of mixed learning abilities, mixed modality strengths, mixed language proficiency, and mixed cultural backgrounds, for the most successful teaching, the integration of learning modalities is a must.

Learning Style Is *Not* an Indicator of Intelligence but of How a Person Learns

Related to learning modality is learning style, which can be defined as *independent forms of knowing and processing information.* While some older children may be comfortable with beginning their learning of a new idea in the abstract (e.g., visual or verbal symbolization—for example, returning to the Classroom Vignette, the chemistry teacher merely gives a lecture with perhaps some chalkboard visuals about the discovery of oxygen), most need to begin with the concrete (e.g., learning by actually doing it). Many students prosper while working in groups, while others prefer to work alone. Some are quick in their studies, whereas others are slow and methodical and cautious and meticulous. Some can sustain attention on a single topic for a long time, becoming more absorbed in their study as time passes. Others are slower starters and more casual in their pursuits but are capable of shifting with ease from subject to subject. Some can study in the midst of music, noise, or movement, whereas others need quiet, solitude, and a desk or table. The point is this: *Students vary not only in their skills and preferences in the way knowledge is received, but also in how they mentally process that information once it has been received.* This latter is a person's style of learning.

It is important to understand that *learning style is not an indicator of intelligence, but rather an indicator of how a person learns.* Although, and as implied in the preceding paragraph, there are probably as many types of learning styles as there are individuals, Kolb describes two major differences in how people learn: how they perceive situations and how they process information (Kolb, 1984). On the basis of perceiving and processing and the earlier work of Carl Jung (Jung, 1923), Bernice McCarthy (1997) describes four major learning styles:

1. The *imaginative learner* perceives information concretely and processes it reflectively. Imaginative learners learn well by listening and sharing with others, integrating the ideas of others with their own experiences. Imaginative learners often have difficulty adjusting to traditional teaching, which depends less on classroom interactions and students' sharing and connecting of their prior experiences. In a traditional classroom, the imaginative learner is likely to be an at-risk student.

2. The *analytic learner* perceives information abstractly and processes it reflectively. The analytic learner prefers sequential thinking, needs details, and values what experts have to offer. Analytic learners do well in traditional classrooms.

3. The *commonsense learner* perceives information abstractly and processes it actively. Commonsense learners are pragmatic and enjoy hands-on learning. They sometimes find school frustrating unless they can see immediate use to

what is being learned. In the traditional classroom, the commonsense learner is likely to be a learner who is at risk of not completing school, of dropping out.

4. The *dynamic learner* perceives information concretely and processes it actively. The dynamic learner prefers hands-on learning and is excited by anything new. Dynamic learners are risk takers and are frustrated by learning if they see it as being tedious and sequential. In a traditional classroom, the dynamic learner also is likely to be an at-risk student.

The Learning Cycle

To understand conceptual development and change, researchers in the 1960s developed a Piaget-based theory of learning, where students are guided from concrete, hands-on learning experiences to the abstract formulations of concepts and their formal applications. This theory became known as the three-phase learning cycle (Karplus, 1974). Long a popular strategy for teaching science, the learning cycle can be useful in other disciplines as well (see Rule, 1995 and Sowell, 1993). The three phases are (1) the *exploratory hands-on phase*, where students can explore ideas and experience assimilation and disequilibrium that lead to their own questions and tentative answers; (2) the *invention* or *concept development phase*, where, under the guidance of the teacher, students invent concepts and principles that help them answer their questions and reorganize their ideas (that is, the students revise their thinking to allow the new information to fit); and (3) the *expansion* or *concept application phase*, another hands-on phase, where the students try out their new ideas by applying them to situations that are relevant and meaningful to them. During application of a concept, the learner may discover new information that causes a change in the learner's understanding of the concept being applied. Thus, the process of learning is cyclical.

There have been more recent interpretations or modifications of the three-phase cycle, such as McCarthy's 4MAT. With the 4MAT system, teachers employ a learning cycle of instructional strategies to try and reach each student's learning style. As stated by McCarthy, in the cycle, learners "sense and feel, they experience, then they watch, they reflect, then they think, they develop theories, then they try out theories, they experiment. Finally, they evaluate and synthesize what they have learned in order to apply it to their next similar experience. They get smarter. They apply experience to experiences" (McCarthy, 1990). And in this process, they are likely to be using all four learning modalities.

To evince *constructivist learning theory*, that is, that learning is a process involving the active engagement of learners, who adapt the educative event to fit, and expand, their individual world view (as opposed to the behaviorist pedagogical assumption that learning is something done to learners) (DeLay, 1996) and to accentuate the importance of student self-assessment, some recent variations of the learning cycle include a fourth phase, an "assessment phase." However, because I believe that assessment of what students know or think they know should be a continual process, permeating all three phases of the learning cycle, I reject any treatment of "assessment" as a self-standing phase.

Learning Capacities

In contrast to four learning styles, Gardner introduces what he calls "learning capacities" exhibited by individuals in differing ways (Gardner, 1996; *Educational Leadership,* September 1997). Originally and sometimes still referred to as multiple intelligences, capacities thus far identified are the following:

Bodily/kinesthetic: ability to use the body skillfully and to handle objects skillfully

Interpersonal: ability to understand people and relationships

Intrapersonal: ability to assess one's emotional life as a means to understand oneself and others

Logical/mathematical: ability to handle chains of reasoning and to recognize patterns and orders

Musical: sensitivity to pitch, melody, rhythm, and tone

Naturalist: ability to draw on materials and features of the natural environment to solve problems or fashion products

Verbal/linguistic: sensitivity to the meaning and order of words

Visual/spatial: ability to perceive the world accurately and to manipulate the nature of space, such as through architecture, mime, or sculpture

It is likely that many of the students who are at risk of not completing school are those who may be dominant in a cognitive learning style that is not in sync with traditional teaching methods. Traditional methods are largely of McCarthy's analytic style, where information is presented in a logical, linear, sequential fashion, and of three of the Gardner types: verbal/linguistic, logical/mathematical, and intrapersonal. Consequently, to better match methods of instruction with learning styles, some teachers and schools have restructured the curriculum and instruction around Gardner's learning capacities. See the following vignette.

TEACHING IN PRACTICE
Using the Theory of Learning Capacities (Multiple Intelligences) and Multilevel Instruction

In a seventh-grade classroom, during one week of a six-week thematic unit on weather, students were concentrating on learning about the water cycle. For this study of the water cycle, with the students' help, the teacher divided the class into several groups of three to five students per group. While working on six projects simultaneously to learn about the water cycle, (1) one group of students designed, conducted, and repeated an experiment to discover the number of drops of water that can be held on one side of a new one-cent coin versus the number that can be held on the side of a worn one-cent coin; (2) working in part with the first group, a second group designed and prepared graphs to illustrate the results of the experiments of the

84

first group; (3) a third group of students created and composed the words and music of a song about the water cycle; (4) a fourth group incorporated their combined interests in mathematics and art to design, collect the necessary materials, and create a colorful and interactive bulletin board about the water cycle; (5) a fifth group read about the water cycle in materials they researched from the Internet and various libraries; and (6) a sixth group created a puppet show about the water cycle. On Friday, the groups shared their completed projects with the whole class.

SUBJECT KNOWLEDGE: FOUNTAINHEAD OF INFORMATION OR AN EDUCATIONAL BROKER?

It is common for beginning teachers to worry that they will be caught by students not knowing something in the subject field that they are teaching. And indeed, sooner or later, you will be caught. But when that happens, perceive it as a teachable moment rather than an embarrassing moment.

Without question, you need to be knowledgeable about the subject content you are being paid to teach. You should have both historical understanding and current knowledge of the structure of that subject content and of the facts, principles, concepts, and skills needed to learn it. This doesn't mean you need to know everything about the subject, but more than you are likely to teach.

Rather than a fountainhead of knowledge, view yourself as an "educational broker." You know where and how to discover information about content you are expected to teach. You cannot know everything there is to know about each subject, but you should become knowledgeable about where and how to best research it and how to assist your students in developing some of those same skills.

Teaching Out of Field

It is amazing and depressing when I learn of yet another first-year secondary school teacher being hired to teach at least part of the time out of his or her major teaching field. Of all persons, the first-year teacher should not have to do this, unless, of course, the teacher has competencies earned in some other way than via university training. The point I am making here is that that first year is demanding enough without having to struggle outside one's subject expertise.

Now, with No Child Left Behind (NCLB) legislation, this should become a problem of decreasing occurrence. So I shall say only that no matter what you teach, but especially if hired to teach all or partly out of your field of expertise, don't be afraid to admit to the students that there are things about the subject that you do not know but that when they arise, you and the students will learn them together. View yourself as not only an educational broker but as an expert on organizing for collaborative learning. See the following vignette.

As a first-year teacher in a rural high school, Alex was the entire science department. In addition to teaching general science, biology, and chemistry, he was responsible for the one class in physics. As a college student, Alex had taken but one year of general physics. And now, as a first-year teacher who had a very limited knowledge of physics, he was absolutely scared to death.

Alex decided that on the first day of class he would level with his students. He told them that he didn't really know much physics, but that he did know how to learn science, how to prepare lab investigations, and how to write test questions. He said the physics he and the students would learn together, collaboratively.

As indeed they did. On the spring statewide test for physics, Alex's students scored in the top quartile of the state. Alex and his physics students were very proud.

SUPPLIES AND TEXTBOOKS: SELDOM IDEAL, SOMETIMES WOEFULLY INADEQUATE

Be prepared for the fact that basic supplies, such as paper, may be inadequate and depleted before the school year ends. Insufficient and/or inadequate teaching supplies is a very real and common problem for beginning teachers (and even veteran teachers), especially for those eager to involve the students in hands-on and minds-on learning.

Teachers find various creative, although seldom permanent and entirely satisfactory, solutions to the problem of shortage of supplies, such as by publishing a wish list and sending it home with the children or sending it out on the school's web page, finding free resources from sources on the Internet, finding less expensive substitute materials, getting help from the parent-teacher organization or a community agency, holding a class fund-raiser such as a car wash, applying for and receiving project grants, and using their own personal funds. Talk with your colleagues about your teaching needs. When it comes to obtaining limited resources from the school administration, an individual teacher is likely to have less clout than will a group of teachers.

It is an unfortunate fact of life that good teachers have to resort to being scavengers and hoarders and to using their own money for the purchase of teaching materials. For a beginning teacher on a skimpy salary, who may still be paying off college loans, this can be a nefarious situation. Please read on!

What You Want for Your Birthday

I readily admit it is presumptuous for me to think that I should be able to tell you what it is that you want this year for your birthday, but please bear with me on this. You may wish to inform relatives and significant others that this year for your birthday and other gift-giving times, you prefer receiving materials and supplies that will enhance your teaching. To that end, you may want to prepare and provide them with a want/need list with sources and prices. For example, perhaps rather than leather luggage, fine jewelry, and a new BMW, you would prefer computer hardware and software, reams of printer paper, construction paper and student scissors, paperback books, a three-hole punch, a filing cabinet, file folders, assorted marking pens, assorted sticky notes, a large bag of crayons, and perhaps items for your professional wardrobe.

Student Textbooks

Generally speaking, students benefit by having their own copies of a textbook and in the latest edition. However, because of budget constraints, this may not always be possible. The book may be outdated; quantities may be limited. When the latter is the case, students may not be allowed to take the books home or perhaps may only occasionally do so. In other classrooms, and even in some schools, by planned design there may be no textbook at all. Yet still, in some classrooms there are two sets of the textbook, one set that remains in the classroom for use there and the other set that is assigned to students to use at home. With that arrangement, students don't have to carry heavy books around in their backpacks. Among schools around the country, unfortunately, and for one reason or another, there are clearly the haves and the have-nots.

Whatever your situation, the following guidelines apply to using the textbook as a learning tool. Progressing through a textbook from the front cover to the back in one school term is not necessarily an indicator of good teaching. The textbook is one resource; to enhance their learning, students should be encouraged to use a variety of resources. Encourage students to search additional sources to update the content of the textbook. This is especially important in certain disciplines such as science and social sciences, where the amount of new information is growing rapidly and student textbooks may be several years old. For the latest information on certain subjects students, should research the library and sources on the Internet. Maintain supplementary reading materials for student use in the classroom. School and community librarians and resource specialists usually are delighted to cooperate with teachers in the selection and provision of such resources.

Consider differentiated reading and personalized assignments in the textbook and supplementary resources (see the discussion of the multireadings approach on the next page). Except to make life simpler for the teacher, there is no advantage in all students working out of the same book and completing only the same exercises. Some students benefit from the drill, practice, and reinforcement afforded by workbooks that accompany textbooks, but this is not true for all students, nor do all benefit from the same activity. In fact, the traditional workbook, now nearly extinct, is being replaced by the modern technology afforded by computer software and DVDs. As the cost of hardware and software programs becomes more realistic for schools, the use of computers by individual students is also becoming more common. Computers and other interactive media provide students with a psychologically safer learning environment in which they have greater control over the pace of the instruction, can repeat instruction if necessary, and can ask for clarification without the fear of embarrassment when having to do so publicly.

To help students develop their higher-level thinking skills and their comprehension of expository material, teach them how to study from their textbook, perhaps by using one of the methods shown in Figure 7.

Figure 7: Methods for developing higher-level thinking skills and comprehension

KQHL: Students ask what they want to know (K) about a topic, list the questions (Q) they need/want answered, ask how (H) they might find answers, and then later identify what they have learned (L) (Long, Drake & Halychyn, 2004).
KWL: Students recall what they already know (K) about a topic, determine what they want to learn (W), and later assess what they have learned (L) (Ogle, 1986).
KWLQ: Students record what they already know (K) about a topic, formulate questions about what they want to learn about the topic (W), search for answers to their questions (L), and ask questions for further study (Q).
POSSE: *predict* ideas, *organize* ideas, *search* for structure, *summarize* main ideas, and *evaluate* understanding (Englert & Mariage, 1991).
PQRST: *preview, question, read, state* the main idea, *and test* yourself by answering the questions you posed earlier (Kelly, 1994).
QAR: Helping learners understand *questions* and *answer* relationships (Mesmer & Hutchins, 2002).
RAP: *read* paragraphs, *ask* questions about what was read, and *put* in own words (Schumaker, Denton, & Deshler, 1984).
Reciprocal teaching: Students are taught and practice the reading skills of summarizing, questioning, clarifying, and predicting (Palincsar & Brown, 1984).
SQ3R: *survey* the chapter, ask *questions* about what was read, *read, recite,* and *review* (Robinson, 1961).
SQ4R: *survey* the chapter, ask *questions* about what was read, *read* to answer the questions, *recite* the answers, *record* important items from the chapter into their notebooks, then *review* it all.
SRQ2R (*survey, read, question, recite, and review*) (Walker, 1995).

Encourage students to be alert for errors in the textbook, both in content and printing, by giving them some sort of credit reward, such as points, when they bring an error to your attention. This helps students develop the skills of critical reading, critical thinking, and healthy skepticism.

Rather than a single textbook approach, some teachers prefer using a *multireadings* strategy that incorporates many readings for a topic during the same unit. The various readings give students a choice in what they read, providing some individualization of instruction by allowing for differences in reading ability and interest level. A teacher-prepared study guide can be used to direct students toward specific information and concepts.

TEACHABLE MOMENTS: BE READY TO RECOGNIZE, CATCH, AND RUN WITH THEM

Casey was teaching an eighth-grade humanities block, a two-hour block course that integrates student learning in social studies, reading, and language arts. On this particular day, while Casey and her students were discussing the topic of Manifest Destiny, one of the students raised a hand and, when acknowledged by Casey, asked, "Why aren't we [referring to the United States] still adding states?" Casey replied immediately with "There aren't any more states to add." By responding too quickly, Casey missed one of those "teachable moments," moments when the teacher has the students right where the teacher wants them, that is, where the students are the ones who are thinking and who are asking intelligent questions. What could Casey have done? When was Hawaii added as a state? Why hasn't Puerto Rico become a state? Guam? etc. Aren't those possibilities? Why aren't more states or territories being added? What are the political and social ramifications today and how do they differ from those of the 1800s? Or even the late 1950s, when Hawaii became a state?

The bottom line? Don't be so lesson plan driven that you are not listening to the students. Be ready to capture and to run with those teachable moments.

The most intellectually demanding tasks lie not so much in solving problems as in posing questions. The kind of schools we need would be staffed by teachers who are as interested in questions students ask after a unit of study as they are in the answers students give.

Elliot W. Eisner (2002)

TEACHER'S LOUNGE: ENTER WITH CAUTION

Teaching can be a highly stressful occupation. Because of that, teachers need sometimes to vent their frustrations. One place they do that is in the teacher's lounge. To avoid being sucked into the frequently negative clime that can permeate a teacher's lounge, you may wisely choose to stay out of it. And when you do hear teachers complaining about students or administrators or parents or colleagues, walk away from the conversation. Surround yourself with only those colleagues who radiate positive energy, avoiding the hearsayers and the naysayers.

TOTAL SCHOOL: ENTER WITH ENTHUSIASM

Knowing that ultimately each and every activity has an effect upon the classroom, you will want to gradually assume an increasing active interest in total school life. The purpose of the school is to serve the education of the students, and the classroom is the primary, but not only, place where this occurs. Every committee meeting, school event, faculty meeting, school board meeting, office, program, and any other planned function that is related to school life shares in the ultimate purpose of better serving the education of the students. Unfortunately, too often adults forget this simple fact. You share in the task of reminding those who do forget.

Student Activities: There Is More to Teaching and Learning Than Classroom Work

There is always need for teachers to help with student activities that extend beyond the classroom, that is, with extracurricular matters, a few of which may offer extra money as incentive for the teacher volunteer. Although involvement in student activities is an excellent way to get to know and to establish rapport with students, beginning teachers sometimes underestimate the amount of time needed for the daily business of teaching, thereby overestimating how much time will remain for extra assignments. During your first year, exercise wisdom and caution when volunteering for or agreeing to assume extra assignments, especially those that involve parents, student travel, or extensive financial matters. For example, being faculty sponsor for the school's chess club is probably less demanding and complicated than is being the faculty supervisor of the school's newspaper or web page.

TRANSITIONS DURING LESSONS: A DIFFICULT SKILL TO MASTER

Transitions are the moments in lessons between activities or topics, times of change. It will probably take you a while to sharpen the skill of smooth transitions. Planning and consistency are important in mastering this important skill. With careful planning, a dependable schedule, and consistent routines, transitions usually occur efficiently and automatically, without disruption. Still, it is probable that for classroom teachers the greatest number of control problems occur during times of transitions, especially when students must wait for the next activity. To avoid problems during transitions, eliminate wait times by thinking and planning ahead. Plan your transitions and write them into your lesson plans.

Transitions in lessons are of two types, and sometimes both are used. One type, called a *lesson transition*, is achieved by the teacher's connecting one activity to the next so that students understand the relationship between the two activities. The second type, called an *anchor* or *transitional activity*, occurs when some students have finished a learning activity but must wait for others to catch up before starting the next. The transitional (or anchor) activity is one intended to keep all students academically occupied, allowing no time where students have nothing to do but wait. A common example is when, during testing, some students finish the test while others have not. The wise and effective teacher plans a transitional activity and gives instructions or reminders for that activity or an ongoing activity before students begin the test.

During the planning phase of instruction, you should plan and rehearse nearly every move you and the students will make during the instructional time, thinking ahead to anticipate and avoid problems in classroom control. Transitions are planned and students are prepared for them by clearly established transition routines. While in transition and waiting for the start of the next activity, students engage in these transitional activities. You can plan a variety of transitional activities relevant and appropriate to the topics being studied, although not necessarily related to the next activity of that particular day's lesson. Depending on the subject being taught and the grade level of your students, transitional activities may include any number of meaningful activities such as journal writing, worksheet activity, lab reports, learning center activity, portfolio work, homework, project work, and even work for another teacher's class.

A useful procedure for writing transitions into your lesson plans is to first outline the procedural section of the lesson plan, designating the various learning activities by consecutive numbering, activity 1, 2, 3, and so on. Then go back over the outline and identify where transitions will occur. After identifying each transition, the next and final step is to plan and write how the transition will be accomplished. For example, if the transition is to move students from whole-class discussion into smaller groups, then the transition should state not only that students will get into small groups but also *how they will do that.* (I highlight the latter because the "how" component of the transition is too often a serious neglect made by beginning teachers.) Or, as another example, if the transition is from a whole-class discussion to viewing a video, describe specifically how the transition will occur. Presumably you will make a statement connecting the just-completed discussion to the content of the upcoming video and related to that you will explain what specifically the students should be looking for as they view the video.

YOUR PLACE OF WORK: SHOW PRIDE IN IT

A drab and uninteresting classroom usually reflects a drab and mind-numbing teacher. To the extent possible, you should make your classroom, that is your place of work, an attractive and functional place to work and in which to learn. Display student work; engage students in planning and organizing classroom displays. Consider the questions shown on the next page.

Does Your Classroom Attractively Display . . .

- Agreed upon classroom rules and procedures, a few major ones?

- Benchmark curriculum standards, the most important ones, with scoring rubrics?

- Helpful information on problem solving and other issues that may cause frequent student questioning?

- Important information about the expected mechanics for writing?

- Photographs of happy and proud students in action—current and past?

- Samples of exemplary student work, including writing and long-term projects?

- Student-created murals and collages that include all students, making each feel he or she belongs?

Your classroom should also be an inviting place for visiting adults. By that I mean, for example, it should have seats for adults. I recall one fifth-grade teacher who had a round table placed near the exit at the rear of the room. Four adult chairs surrounded the table. The table seemed always to be covered with a lovely tablecloth and a fresh flower arrangement. It made for a most inviting and pleasant place for the teacher to meet with visiting parents and other adults. Consider this: a recent study with eighth-grade children suggests that in a classroom atmosphere enhanced with a pleasant fragrance, students require fewer redirections of their behavior from the teacher (Gabriel, 1999). Isn't it worth a try?

TEACHING IN PRACTICE
Joan Makes Significant Changes in Her Classroom Atmosphere

Joan is a fifth-grade teacher of a self-contained classroom. Her classroom consists of one wall in particular that is mostly windows. Until recently she kept the window curtains closed to keep students from being distracted by the outdoors. She heard teachers talking of reports of preliminary studies indicating that children learn mathematics, in particular, better with a background of soft classical music, and in natural lighting rather than in artificial lighting. So now she plays a background of soft classical music when children are learning mathematics, and she keeps the curtains open and the ceiling lights turned off as often as possible. She also heard that some children learn certain subjects better at particular times of the day. So now, rather than teaching each subject at the same time every day, she has established a new weekly schedule that varies the schedule from day to day. Although it is too early to say that student learning in any subject has significantly improved as a result of these changes, Joan has noticed a marked improvement in student behavior, attention, and motivation for learning.

YOUR FIRST OBSERVATION BY THE PRINCIPAL

Along about midyear of your first year of teaching, a school administrator, probably the principal, will observe your teaching during a prearranged classroom visit. This classroom observation will be followed closely by a conference, an evaluation, and the principal's recommendation regarding your reemployment. As a beginning teacher, you undoubtedly will be apprehensive about this ensuing observation and evaluation. Just be prepared, confident, and proud.

Sometimes busy administrators, for one reason or another, must reschedule their visit to your classroom. This notice may come to you at the last minute, after you have carefully and thoughtfully prepared for the visit, both mentally and physically. For a beginning teacher, this can be very disappointing. In my opinion, once an observational visit is scheduled, except for a dire emergency, it should remain paramount in the administrator's schedule. Administrators, unfortunately, often because of the pressures on them, sometimes forget how anxious a beginning teacher can be about the first evaluative observation and ensuing conference.

If you confidently and consistently follow the guidelines and suggestions that have been presented in this little book, the evaluation should go very much in your favor. Use the observational visit as an opportunity to display pride in the work of your students, in your work as a responsible and productive teacher, and in your place of work. Make the most of it, for it will, unfortunately, likely be one of only a handful of times during your entire teaching career that an adult colleague observes you at work.

YOUR PROFESSIONAL PORTFOLIO PLUS PERSONAL RECORDS OF YOUR WORK

Whether or not required in your program of induction, I strongly urge you to maintain your personal professional portfolio (you probably started one while still in teacher training and, perhaps, are maintaining one now for eventual recertification) and records related to your work. The portfolio will likely be useful to you throughout much of your career, probably in some ways you can't now imagine.

Records of your work that I speak of are more for your personal enjoyment not only now but years later. These most often are the little things that happen to a teacher that make the job of teaching so intrinsically rewarding.

For use in continued professional work, I cannot tell you what to put in your portfolio or how to best maintain it, but I urge you on that matter to follow the specific instructions and requirements of your local district and/or state. However, you might find useful one or more of the sources listed in the recommended readings listed on pages 95-99.

EPILOGUE

Teaching is variously referred to as an act of mercy, a performing art, a moral craft, and a science. Surely, good teaching is as much an art as it is a science. There is no magic bag of recipes that one experienced in such matters can pass on to beginners that will always work in every situation. You are a teacher, not a chef. Starting now and continuing throughout your career, you will try your own ideas and you will borrow and modify ideas from others. You will continue to discover what works best for you in your own distinct situation with your own unique sets of students and challenges.

As a teacher, you are a learner among learners. You continue your journey of self-discovery, from student to student teacher to beginning classroom teacher to veteran teacher. The transition you have made to the first year of teaching is the beginning of an important career, during which you will be in a perpetual mode of reflection and learning. At this time, and as I said in the prologue, you should not expect mastery from yourself. Rather, establish some realistic and achievable goals for yourself and then work toward those goals, periodically reflecting and self-assessing on both what and how you are doing. Experience and learn, and before you know it, you will be recognized by your students, parents, and colleagues as a master teacher.

I am indeed indebted and exceedingly grateful to all the people in my life, now and in the past, who have interacted with me and reinforced what I have felt since the days I first began my career as teacher: Teaching is the most rewarding profession of all. I truly wish the best to you for what can be a long-lasting and very rewarding career.

Richard D. Kellough

REFERENCES AND RECOMMENDED READINGS

Allen, R. (2003). An early taste of college: Accelerated learning with support motivates urban students. *Education Update, 45,* 1, 3, & 8.

Anguiano, P. (2001). A first-year teacher's plan to reduce misbehavior in the classroom. *Teaching Exceptional Children, 33*(3), 52-55.

Beck, C. R. (2001). Matching teaching strategies to learning style preferences. *Teacher Educator 37*(1), 1-15.

Beck, R. J., Livne, N. L., & Bear, S. L. (2005). Teachers' self-assessment of formative and summative electronic portfolios on professional development. *European Journal of Teacher Education, 28,* 221-224.

Bobeck, B. L. (2002). Teacher resiliency: A key to career longevity. *Clearing House, 75,* 202-205.

Bolland, J. M. (2003). Hopelessness and risk behaviour among adolescents living in high-poverty inner-city neighbourhoods." *Journal of Adolescence, 26,* 145-158.

Brighton, C. M. (2002). Straddling the fence: Implementing best practices in an age of accountability. *Gifted Child Today Magazine, 25*(3), 30-33.

Bromfield, R. (2003). *Handle with care: Understanding children and teachers.* New York: Teachers College Press.

Brookhart, S. M. (2004). *Grading.* Upper Saddle River, NJ: Merrill Prentice Hall.

Burmark, L., & Fournier, L. (2003). *Enlighten up! An educator's guide to stress-free living.* Alexandria, VA: Association for Supervision and Curriculum Development.

Conn, K. (2002). *The Internet and the law: What educators need to know.* Alexandria, VA: Association for Supervision and Curriculum Development.

Conway, C., Hansen, E, Schulz, A., Stimson, J., & Wozniak-Reese, J. (2004). Becoming a teacher: Stories of the first few years." *Music Educators Journal, 91*(1), 45.

Cookson, P. W., Jr. (2005a). The challenge of isolation. Professional development— Your first year. *Teaching Pre K-8, 36*(2), 14 & 16.

Cookson, P. W., Jr. (2005b). Your first year: A teacher's journey. *Teaching Pre K-8, 35*(8), 12-13.

Costa, A. L. (1991). *The school as a home for the mind.* Palatine, IL: Skylight Publishing.

DeLay, R. (1996). Forming knowledge: Constructivist learning and experiential education. *Journal of Experiential Education, 19*(2), 76-81.

Dobbs, C. L. (2002). New teacher nerves. *Journal of Adolescent & Adult Literacy, 45,* 540-542.

Dunn, R. (1995). *Strategies for educating diverse learners.* Fastback 384. Bloomington, IN: Phi Delta Kappa Educational Foundation.

Educational Leadership theme issue. (1997). Teaching for multiple intelligences, *55(1).*

Eisner, E. W. (2002). The kind of schools we need. *Phi Delta Kappan, 84,* 579.

Englert, C. S., & Mariage, T. V. (1991). Making students partners in the comprehension process: Organizing the reading "POSSE." *Learning Disability Quarterly, 14*(1), 123-138 .

Ertmer, P. A., Hruskocy, C., & Woods, D. M. (2003). *Education on the Internet: The worldwide classroom: Access to people, resources, and curriculum connections.* Upper Saddle River, NJ: Merrill Prentice Hall.

Feiman-Nemser, S. (2003). What new teachers need to learn. *Educational Leadership, 60*(8), 25-29.

Fitzgerald, J., & Graves, M. F. (2005). Reading supports for all. *Educational Leadership, 62*(4), 68-71.

Foster, A. S. (2003). Let the dogs out: Using bobble head toys to explore force and motion. *Science Scope, 26*(7), 16-19.

Frost, R., Olson, E., & Valiquette, L. (2000). The wolf pack: Power shared and power earned—building a middle school nation. *Middle School Journal, 31*(5), 30-36.

Gabriel, A. E. (1999) Brain-based learning: The scent of the trail." *Clearing House, 72,* 288-290.

Gardner, H. (1996). Multiple intelligences: Myths and messages. *International Schools Journal, 15*(2): 8-22.

Georgiady, N. P., & Romano, L. G. (2002). *Positive parent-teacher conferences.* Fastback 491. Bloomington, IN: Phi Delta Kappa Educational Foundation.

Good, T. L., & Brophy, J. E. (2003). *Looking in classrooms, 9*th ed. New York: Addison Wesley Longman.

Goodnough, K. (2000). Humble advice for new science teachers. *Science Scope, 23*(6): 20-24.

Heath, M. (2005). Are you ready to go digital?: The pros and cons of electronic portfolio development. *Library Media Connection, 23*(7):66.

Hinton-Johnson, K. (2002). In the process of becoming multicultural: Reflections of a first year teacher. *New Advocate, 15,* 309-313.

Horton, M. L. (2004). Digital portfolios in physical education teacher preparation. *Journal of Physical Education Recreation and Dance, 75*(9), 35.

Hunt, T. J., & Hunt, B. (2003). Contradictions and Confidence: Reflections on being the new experts. *English Journal, 93*(1), 92-95.

Jarolimek, J., Foster, C. D. Sr., & Kellough, R. D. (2005). *Teaching and learning in the elementary school.* 8th ed. Upper Saddle River, NJ: Merrill Prentice Hall.

Jung, C. G. (1923). *Psychological types.* New York: Harcourt Brace.

Karplus, R. (1974). *Science curriculum improvement study.* Teacher's Handbook. Berkeley: University of California.

Kellough, R. D. (1970). The humanistic approach: An experiment in the teaching of biology to slow learners in high school—an experiment in classroom experimentation. *Science Education, 54,* 253-262.

Kellough, R. D. (2007). *A resource guide for teaching K-12.* 5th ed. Upper Saddle River, NJ: Merrill Prentice Hall.

Kellough, R. D., & Carjuzaa, J. (2006) *Teaching in the middle and secondary schools.* 8th ed. Upper Saddle River, NJ: Merrill Prentice Hall.

Kellough, R. D., & Kellough, N. G. (2007). *Secondary school teaching: A guide to methods and resources.* 3d ed. Upper Saddle River, NJ: Merrill Prentice Hall.

Kellough, R. D., & Kellough, N. G. (2008). *Teaching young adolescents: A guide to methods and resources.* 5th ed. Upper Saddle River, NJ: Merrill Prentice Hall.

Kellough, R. D., et al. (1996). *Integrating language arts and social studies for intermediate and middle school students.* Upper Saddle River, NJ: Merrill Prentice Hall.

Kellough, R. D., et al. (1996). *Integrating mathematics and science for intermediate and middle school students.* Upper Saddle River, NJ: Merrill Prentice Hall.

Kellough, R. D., et al. (1996). *Integrating mathematics and science for kindergarten and primary children.* Upper Saddle River, NJ: Merrill Prentice Hall.

Kelly, E. B. (1994). *Memory enhancement for educators.* Bloomington, IN: Fastback 365, Phi Delta Kappa Educational Foundation.

Klenowski, V., Askew, S., & Carnell, E. (2006). Portfolios for learning, assessment, and professional development in higher education. *Assessment & Evaluation in Higher Education, 31,* 267-286.

Kolb, D. A. (1984). *Experiential learning: Experience as a source of learning and development.* Upper Saddle River, NJ: Prentice Hall.

Kwame-Ross, T. (2003). In just a minute: Teaching students the skills of waiting. *Responsive Classroom, 15,* 1, 4-5.

Lemkuhl, M. (2002). Pen-pal letters: The cross-curricular experience. *Reading Teacher, 55,* 720-722.

Lindbolm, K. & Bush, J. (2005). Teaching English in the world. *English Journal, 95*(2), 105.

Long, D., Drake, K., & Halychyn, D. (2004). Go on a science quest. *Science & Children, 42*(2), 40-45.

Lovingood, K. (2004). National certification: One teachers' experience. *Music Educators Journal, 91*(2), 19.

MacBain, D. E. (1996). *Intergenerational education programs.* Fastback 402. Bloomington, IN: Phi Delta Kappa Educational Foundation.

Marzano, R. J. (2003). *Classroom management that works: Research-based strategies for every teacher.* Alexandria, VA: Association for Supervision and Curriculum Development.

May, H. (June 11, 2001). High, lows mark teacher's first year. *The Salt Lake Tribune.*

McCarthy, B. & McCarthy, D. (2006). *Teaching around the 4MAT cycle.* Thousand Oaks, CA: Corwin Press.

McCarthy, B. (1990). Using the 4MAT system to bring learning styles to schools. *Educational Leadership, 48*(2), 33.

McCarthy, B. (1997). A tale of four learners: 4MAT's learning styles. *Educational Leadership, 54*(6), 47-51.

McCarty, P., Ostrem, J., & Young, P. (2004). Saving teachers' voices. *Principal, 82*(2), 56-57.

McCarty, P., Ostrem, J., & Young, P. (2004). Saving teachers' voices. *Principal, 82*(2), 56-57.

Mesmer, H. A. E., & Hutchins. E. J. (2002). Using QARs with charts and graphs. *Reading Teacher, 56,*(1), 21-27.

Meyer, L. (Autumn 2000). Barriers to meaningful instruction for English learners. *Theory into Practice,* 228-236.

Miller, P. C., & Endo, H. (2004). Understanding and meeting the needs of ESL students. *Phi Delta Kappan 85,* 786-791.

Ness, M. (2001). Lessons of a first-year teacher. *Phi Delta Kappan, 82*, 700-701.

Normore, A. H., & Floyd, A. (2005). A roller coaster ride: The twists and turns of a novice teacher's relationship with her principal. *Phi Delta Kappan, 86*, 767-771.

Ogle, D. M. (1986). K-W-L: A teaching model that develops active reading of expository text. *Reading Teacher, 39*, 564-570.

Palincsar, A. S., & Brown, A. L. (1984). Reciprocal teaching of comprehension-fostering and comprehension-monitoring activities. *Cognition and Instruction, 1,* 117-175.

Pardini, P. (2002). Stitching new teachers into the school's fabric. *Journal of Staff Development, 23*(3), 23-26.

Pauly, E. (2002-2003). No one told me about May. *Journal of Adolescent & Adult Literacy, 46*, 284-287.

Pope, S. (2002). Journal reflections of a first-year teacher. *Learning Languages*, 7(2), 8-10.

Rathjen, D. (2001). Change is a constant. *Primary Voices K-6* 9(3), 22-30.

Reese. S. (2004). Teacher portfolios: Displaying the art of teaching. *Techniques: Connecting Education and Careers, 79*(5), 18-21.

Reiss, J. (2001). *ESOL strategies for teaching content: Facilitating instruction for English language learners.* Upper Saddle River, NJ: Merrill Prentice Hall.

Roberts, P. L., & Kellough, R. D. (2008). *A guide for developing an interdisciplinary thematic unit.* 4th ed. Upper Saddle River, NJ: Merrill Prentice Hall.

Roberts, P. L., Kellough, R. D., & Moore, K. (2006). *A resource guide for elementary school teaching: Planning for competence.* 6th ed. Upper Saddle River, NJ: Merrill Prentice Hall.

Robinson, F. P. (1961). *Effective study* (rev. ed.). New York: Harper & Brothers.

Rossi, R. J., & Stringfield, S. C. (1995). What we must do for students placed at risk. *Phi Delta Kappan, 77,* 73-76.

Rule, A. C. (1995). *Using the learning cycle to teach acronyms, a language arts lesson.* ED383000.

Schlichte, J,, Yssel, N., & Merbler, J. (2005). Pathways to burnout: Case studies in teacher isolation and alienation. *Preventing School Failure, 50,* 35.

Schroeder-Arce, R. (2002). Walking on ice: Facing cultural and lingual challenges as an 'other'. *Stage of the Art,*14(3), 22-24.

Schumaker , J. B., Denton, P. H., & Deshler, D. D. (1984). *The paraphrasing strategy.* Lawrence, KS: Edge Enterprises.

Shreve, J. (2005). *Let the games begin. Video games, once confiscated in class, are now a key teaching tool. If they're done right.* San Rafael, CA: George Lucas Educational Foundation.

Smoll, T. L. (2004). Fabulous first graders: Confessions of a first-year teacher. *School Arts: The Art Education Magazine for Teachers, 103*(10), 50.

Smyth, T. S. (2005). Respect, reciprocity, and reflection in the classroom. Gateways to experience. *Kappa Delta Pi, 42*(1), 38-41.

Sowell, J. E. (1993). Approach to art history in the classroom. *Art Education, 46*(2), 19-24.

Stein, S. (2001). The tractor and the taxi: Rural and urban students build a new vehicle for friendship in an Internet mural project. *Teaching Tolerance, 19,* 30-33.

Thompson, J. G. (2003). *The first year teacher's survival kit.* Bloomington, IN: Phi Delta Kappa International.

Tiedt, P. I., & I. M. Tiedt. (1995). *Multicultural teaching: A handbook of activities, information, and resources.* 4th ed. Boston: Allyn & Bacon.

Victor, E., & Kellough, R. D. (2004). *Science K-8: An integrated approach.* 10th ed. Upper Saddle River, NJ: Merrill Prentice Hall.

Walker, M. L. (1995). Help for the 'fourth-grade slump'—SRQ2R plus instruction in text structure or main idea." *Reading Horizons, 36*(1), 38-58.

Walling, D. R. (1993). *English as a second language: 25 questions and answers.* Fastback 347. Bloomington, IN: Phi Delta Kappa Educational Foundation.

Weasmer, J. (2002). A gift of time: Career history of a late-entry teacher. *Clearing House 75*, 218-221.

Weber, E. (2005). *MI Strategies in the Classroom and Beyond.* Boston: Pearson Allyn & Bacon.

Wilcox, E. (2003). A mid-career teacher's juggling act. *Teaching Music, 10*(4), 28-33.

Wood, J. M. (2000). Innovative teachers hindered by the 'green-eyed monster'. *Harvard Education Letter, 16*(4), 8 & 7.

Worthy, J. (2005). It didn't have to be so hard: The first years of teaching in an urban school. *International Journal of Qualitative Studies in Education, 18*, 379-398.

GLOSSARY

ability grouping The assignment of students to separate classrooms or to separate activities within a classroom according to their perceived academic abilities. Homogeneous grouping is the grouping of students of similar abilities; heterogeneous grouping is the grouping of students of mixed abilities.

accountability Reference to the concept that an individual is responsible for his or her behaviors and should be able to demonstrate publicly the worth of the activities carried out.

affective domain The area of learning related to interests, attitudes, feelings, values, and personal adjustment.

alternative assessment Assessment of learning in ways that are different from traditional paper-and-pencil objective testing, such as a portfolio, project, or self-assessment. See also *authentic assessment.*

assessment The relatively neutral process of finding out what students are or have learned as a result of instruction.

at-risk General term given to a student who shows a high potential for not completing school.

authentic assessment The use of assessment procedures (usually portfolios and projects) that are highly compatible with the instructional objectives. Also referred to as *accurate, active, aligned, alternative, direct,* and *performance assessment.*

basal reader A reading textbook designed for a specific grade level.

behavioral objective A statement of expectation describing what the learner should be able to do upon completion of the instruction.

behaviorism A theory that equates learning with changes in observable behavior.

classroom control The process of influencing student behavior in the classroom.

classroom management The teacher's system of establishing a climate for learning, including techniques for preventing and handling student misbehavior.

coaching See *mentoring.*

cognitive domain The area of learning related to intellectual skills, such as retention and assimilation of knowledge.

cognitivism A theory that holds that learning entails the construction or reshaping of mental schemata and that mental processes mediate learning. Also known as *constructivism.*

comprehension A level of cognition that refers to the skill of understanding.

constructivism See *cognitivism.*

convergent thinking Thinking that is directed to a preset conclusion.

cooperative learning A genre of instructional strategies that use small groups of students working together and helping each other on learning tasks, stressing support for one another rather than competition.

core curriculum Subject or discipline components of the curriculum considered as being absolutely necessary. Traditionally these are English/language arts, mathematics, science, and social science.

criterion A standard by which behavioral performance is judged.

criterion-referenced assessment Assessment in which standards are established and behaviors are judged against the present guideline, rather than against the behaviors of others.

critical thinking The ability to recognize and identify problems, to propose and to test solutions, and to arrive at tentative conclusions based on the data collected.

curriculum Originally derived from a Latin term referring to a racecourse for the chariots the term still has no widely accepted definition. As used in this text, curriculum is that which is planned and encouraged for teaching and learning. This includes both school and nonschool environments, overt (formal) and hidden (informal) curriculums, and broad as well as narrow notions of content—its development, acquisition, and consequences.

deductive learning Learning that proceeds from the general to the specific. See also *expository learning.*

diagnostic assessment See *preassessment.*

didactic teaching See *direct instruction.*

differentiated instruction Varying the methods and content of instruction according to individual student differences and needs. See also *individualized instruction.*

direct experience Learning by doing (applying) what is being learned.

direct instruction Teacher-centered expository instruction, such as lecturing or a teacher-guided group discussion.

direct intervention Teacher use of verbal reminders or verbal commands to redirect student behavior, as opposed to nonverbal gestures or cues.

discipline The process of controlling student behavior in the classroom. The term has been largely replaced by the terms *classroom control* or *classroom management.* It is also used in reference to the subject taught (e.g., language arts, science, mathematics, and so forth).

discovery learning Learning that proceeds from identification of a problem, through the development of hypotheses, the testing of the hypotheses, and the arrival at a conclusion. See also *critical thinking.*

divergent thinking Thinking that expands beyond original thought.

early adolescence The developmental stage of young people as they approach and begin to experience puberty. This stage usually occurs between 10 and 14 years of age and deals with the successful attainment of the appropriate developmental characteristics for this age span.

effective school A school where students master basic skills, seek academic excellence in all subjects, demonstrate achievement, and display good behavior and attendance. Known also as an *exemplary school.*

elementary school Any school that has been planned and organized especially for children of some combination of grades K-6. There are many variations, though; for example, a school might house children of preschool through seven or eight and still be called an elementary school.

empathy The ability to understand the feelings of another person.

equality Considered to be the same in status or competency level.

equity Fairness and justice, that is, impartiality.

evaluation Like assessment, but includes making sense out of the assessment results, usually based on criteria or a rubric. Evaluation is more subjective than is assessment.

expository learning The traditional classroom instructional approach that proceeds as follows: presentation of information to the learners, reference to particular examples, and application of the information to the learner's experiences.

extrinsic motivators Motivation of learning by rewards outside the learner, such as parent and teacher expectations, gifts, certificates, stamps, and grades.

facilitating behavior Teacher behavior that makes it possible for students to learn.

formative evaluation Evaluation of learning in progress.

goal, course A broad generalized statement about the expected outcomes of a course.

hands-on learning Learning by actively doing.

heterogeneous grouping A grouping pattern that does not separate students into groups based on their intelligence, learning achievement, or physical characteristics.

high school A school that houses students in any combination of grades 9–12.

high-stakes assessment Any assessment that has highly consequential outcomes for students, teachers, and schools. Highly consequential outcomes may include any or all of the following: student placement in groups, retention or promotion, school-funding decisions, tagging of schools as successful or failing.

homogeneous grouping A grouping pattern that separates students into groups based on common characteristics, such as intelligence, achievement, or physical characteristics.

inclusion The commitment to the education of each special-needs learner, to the maximum extent appropriate, in the school and classroom the student would otherwise attend.

indirect instruction Student-centered teaching using discovery and inquiry as learning strategies.

individualized instruction The self-paced process whereby individual students assume responsibility for learning through study, practice, feedback, and reinforcement with appropriately designed instructional modules. See also *differentiated instruction.*

inductive learning Learning that proceeds from specifics to the general. See also *discovery learning.*

inquiry learning Like discovery learning, except the learner designs the processes to be used in resolving the problem.

instruction Planned arrangement of experiences to help a learner develop understanding and to achieve a desirable change in behavior.

integrated curriculum Curriculum organization that combines subject matter traditionally taught independently.

interdisciplinary instruction Instruction that combines subject matter disciplines traditionally taught independently.

interdisciplinary team An organizational pattern of two or more teachers representing different subject areas. The team shares the same students, schedule, areas of the school, and the opportunity for teaching more than one subject.

interdisciplinary thematic unit (ITU) A thematic unit that crosses boundaries of two or more disciplines.

intermediate grades Term sometimes used to refer to grades 4-6.

internalization The extent to which an attitude or value becomes a part of the learner. That is, without having to think about it, the learner's behavior reflects the attitude or value.

intervention A teacher's interruption to redirect a student's behavior, either by direct intervention (e.g., by a verbal command) or by indirect intervention (e.g., by eye contact or physical proximity).

intrinsic motivation Motivation of learning through the student's internal sense of accomplishment.

intuition Knowing without conscious reasoning.

junior high school A school that houses grades 7–9 or 7–8 and that has a schedule and curriculum that resemble those of the senior high school (grades 9–12 or 10–12) more than they do those of the elementary school.

learning The development of understandings and the change in behavior resulting from experiences.

learning center (LC) An instructional strategy that utilizes activities and materials located at a special place in the classroom and that is designed to allow a student to work independently at his or her own pace to learn one area of content.

learning modality The way a person receives information. Four modalities are recognized: visual, auditory, tactile (touch), and kinesthetic (movement).

learning style The way a person learns best in a given situation.

looping An arrangement in which the cohort of students and teachers remain together as a group for several or for all the years a child is at a particular school. Also referred to as *multiyear grouping, multiyear instruction, multiyear placement,* and *teacher-student progression.*

magnet school A school that specializes in a particular academic area, such as science, mathematics and technology, the arts, or international relations. Also referred to as a *theme school.*

mastery learning The concept that a student should master the content of one lesson before moving on to the content of the next.

measurement The process of collecting and interpreting data.

mentoring One-on-one coaching, tutoring, or guidance to facilitate learning.

metacognition Planning, monitoring, and evaluating one's own thinking. Known also as *reflective abstraction.*

middle grades Grades 5–8.

middle school A school that has been planned and organized especially for students of ages 10-14.

minds-on learning Learning in which the learner is intellectually active, thinking about what is being learned.

modeling The teacher's direct and indirect demonstration, by actions and by words, of the behaviors expected of students.

multilevel teaching See *multitasking.*

multimedia The combined use of sound, video, and graphics for instruction.

multiple intelligences A theory of several different intelligences, as opposed to just one general intelligence; intelligences that have been described are verbal/linguistic, musical, logical/mathematical, naturalist, visual/spatial, bodily/kinesthetic, interpersonal, and intrapersonal.

multitasking The simultaneous use of several levels of teaching and learning in the same classroom, with students working on different objectives or different tasks leading to the same objective. Also known as *multilevel teaching.*

overt behavior A behavior that is outwardly observable.

peer tutoring An instructional strategy that places students in a tutorial role in which one student helps another learn.

performance assessment See *authentic assessment.*

performance-based instruction Instruction designed around the instruction and assessment of student achievement against specified and predetermined objectives.

portfolio assessment An alternative approach to evaluation that assembles representative samples of a student's work over time as a basis for assessment.

positive reinforcer A means of encouraging desired student behaviors by rewarding those behaviors when they occur.

preassessment Diagnostic assessment of what students know or think they know prior to the instruction.

procedure A statement telling the student how to accomplish a task.

psychomotor domain The domain of learning that involves locomotor behaviors.

reciprocal teaching A form of collaborative teaching where the teacher and the students share the teaching responsibility and all are involved in asking questions, clarifying, predicting, and summarizing.

reflection The conscious process of mentally replaying experiences.

reflective abstraction See *metacognition.*

reliability In measurement, the consistency with which an item or instrument is measured over time.

rubric An outline of the criteria used to assess a student's work.

secondary school Traditionally, any school housing students for any combination of grades 7–12.

self-contained classroom Commonly used in the primary grades, it is a grouping pattern where one teacher teaches all or almost all subjects to one group of children.

senior high school Usually a high school that houses only students in grades 9-12 or 10-12.

simulation An abstraction or simplification of a real-life situation.

summative assessment Assessment of learning after instruction is completed.

teaching See *instruction*.

teaching style The way teachers teach; their distinctive mannerisms complemented by their choices of teaching behaviors and strategies.

teaching team A team of two or more teachers who work together to provide instruction to the same group of students, either alternating the instruction or team teaching simultaneously.

team teaching Two or more teachers working together to provide instruction to a group of students.

tenured teacher After serving a designated number of years in the same school district (usually three) as a probationary teacher, upon rehire the teacher receives a tenure contract, which means that the teacher is automatically rehired each year thereafter unless the contract is revoked by either the district or the teacher and for specific and legal reasons.

thematic unit A unit of instruction built on a central theme or concept.

think time See *wait time*.

tracking The practice of the voluntary or involuntary placement of students in different programs or courses according to their ability and prior academic performance.

transition In a lesson, the planned procedures that move student thinking from one idea to the next or that move their actions from one activity to the next. With reference to schooling, transitions are the times when a student moves from one level of school to the next.

validity In measurement, the degree to which an item or instrument measures that which it is intended to measure.

wait time In the use of questioning, the period of silence between the time a question is asked and the inquirer (teacher) does something, such as repeats the question, rephrases the question, calls on a particular student, answers the question him- or herself, or asks another question. Also known as *think time*.

withitness The teacher's timely ability to intervene and redirect a student's inappropriate behavior.

INDEX